Lost Buildings of Britain

By the Same Author

Henry VIII: Images of a Tudor King
The Royal Palaces of Tudor England
Whitehall Palace
Hampton Court: A Social and
Architectural History

Lost Buildings
of Britain

SIMON THURLEY

VIKING
an imprint of
PENGUIN BOOKS

VIKING

Published by the Penguin Group
Penguin Books Ltd, 80 Strand, London WC2R 0RL, England
Penguin Group (USA), Inc., 375 Hudson Street, New York, New York 10014, USA
Penguin Books Australia Ltd, 250 Camberwell Road, Camberwell, Victoria 3124, Australia
Penguin Books Canada Ltd, 10 Alcorn Avenue, Toronto, Ontario, Canada M4V 3B2
Penguin Books India (P) Ltd, 11 Community Centre, Panchsheel Park, New Delhi – 110 017, India
Penguin Group (NZ), cnr Airborne and Rosedale Roads, Albany, Auckland 1310, New Zealand
Penguin Books (South Africa) (Pty) Ltd, 24 Sturdee Avenue, Rosebank 2196, South Africa

Penguin Books Ltd, Registered Offices: 80 Strand, London WC2R 0RL, England

www.penguin.com

First published 2004
1

Set in 12/14.75 pt Monotype Bembo
Typeset by Rowland Phototypesetting Ltd, Bury St Edmunds, Suffolk
Printed in Great Britain by Clays Ltd, St Ives plc

A CIP catalogue record for this book is available from the British Library

ISBN 0-670-91521-1

for Katharine

Contents

List of Illustrations

Black and White Illustrations

Acknowledgements

This book came out of a television series for Channel 4, made by Darlow Smithson Productions. It was their idea and I must thank John Smithson, Alice Keens Soper and Ian Holt and Jenni Butterworth for it. In making the programmes we benefited from a galaxy of talent. All the following helped clarify my views about the six lost buildings: for Fonthill Abbey, Dr Megan Aldrich, Professor John Ashurst, Dr Stephen Calloway, Dr Philippa Glanville, Philip Hewat-Jaboor, Amy Frost and Keith Weston; for Whitehall Palace, Professor Robert Bucholz, Chris Thomas, Dr Andrew Barclay, Dr Thomas Cocke, Adriana Turpin, Michael Green and Dr Anna Keay; for Nottingham Castle, Professor Philip Dixon, Dr John Goodall, Dr Pamela Marshall, Dr Trevor Foulds, Andrew Robertshaw, Stuart Prior and Dr Sally Dixon-Smith; for Millbank Penitentiary, Alan Brodie, Professor Sean McConville, Mark Burbidge, Ned Crowe, Dr Joanna Adler, Karl Hulker, Dr Stephen Duchar and Dr Richard Ireland; for the Theatre Royal, Drury Lane, Professor Aileen Riberio, Professor David Thomas, Leela Minertas, Dr Gordon Higgott, Dr Cat Fergusson, Professor Christopher Baugh, David Wilmore, Andrew Westman and Jason Watkins; for Glastonbury Abbey, Glyn Coppack, Tim Tatton-Brown, Jerry Samson, Professor Roberta Gilchrist, Professor Philip Lindley, Dr James Clarke, Jill Channer and Hazel Forsyth. I would also like to thank the crew and directors of the films for asking difficult questions that made me look at the sites in a different way. This book benefited enormously from the comments of my editor at Penguin, Kate Barker, and from the sharp eye of Jane Birdsell.

Introduction

On most days on my way to the office I walk through Trafalgar Square, past the fountains and the enormous bronze lions. Sometimes I look up to the statue of Nelson perched high above the traffic and wonder what it would be like if he were not there. It is almost impossible to imagine central London without Nelson's Column. It would be just as difficult walking down Princes Street in Edinburgh to imagine the city without the castle, or in Newcastle the Tyne Gorge without the bridges, or in Liverpool the Pier Head without the Liver Building. It would be odd to watch a prime ministerial announcement without the backdrop of the front door of 10 Downing Street or to see in the new year without the chimes of Big Ben. Do we want Brighton without the Palace Pier, Blackpool without its tower, Salisbury without its cathedral or Caernarfon without its castle? I guess for almost everyone the answer is no. These great buildings give our cities and towns a sense of identity and history: they remind us who we are and where we have come from. But for every great monument that survives, a hundred have gone. British history is a catalogue of lost buildings, structures that were once as integral to people's everyday lives as Nelson's Column, Edinburgh Castle and the Liver Building are now. Some are ruins, some are just memories in the street pattern, and of others there is no trace at all.

Finding lost buildings has been an obsession throughout my life. My search started as a child in a hole dug in my parents' garden in Godmanchester, Cambridgeshire. Godmanchester was founded by the Romans at the point where the great Roman north road, Ermine Street crossed the River Ouse. A fort was built there within years of the Claudian invasion of AD 43 as part of a network of forts and roads designed to suppress the ancient British tribe of the Catuvellanians. Like so many other East Anglian Roman towns it was destroyed by Queen Boudicca in her uprising of AD 60 but was quickly rebuilt and became an important stopping-off point for people moving north and south. In the second century it became quite prosperous and in about AD 120 a *mansio* or inn was built as a rest house for travellers on Ermine Street. A bathhouse was built next door, and I remember as a small boy being taken down to a neighbour's garden by my parents to see the archaeologist Michael Green excavating this large and imposing structure. Thanks to Michael's fondness for children, my sister and I would be left at the side of the spoil heaps to wash pots and watch the progress of the excavation. When my mother visited and Michael explained to her the layers of earth, the post holes, the walls and pits, we would peer over the edge, not getting too close for fear of falling in, and listen in wonder. Later we would be treated to a preview of the best finds in a site hut.

The *mansio* and baths were the first large Roman structures we saw excavated in Godmanchester. They were impressive buildings. The *mansio* had a stable yard and a large colonnaded inner court with ranges of bedrooms along its east and west sides and a suite of reception rooms on the south. At 100 metres long it was probably the second or third largest building of its type yet found in the UK. Such a find made a strong impression on me and soon after my parents allowed me to excavate a trench in our garden not far away. Ermine Street actually ran beneath the old Baptist manse in which I was brought up and shops and houses must have lain close behind the ditches that lined the road. My first hole was, by chance, sunk directly into a rubbish pit lying at the rear of one of those buildings. Full of pottery, bones, nails, oyster shells and other discarded domestic waste, it was a treasure trove for a nine-year-old. Looking back on this first crude attempt to find out more about the Romans I am faintly horrified. Where was the recording, the careful stratigraphical record, the plotting of the pit? Such things were as remote to me as Rome itself. Yet it inspired a passion to investigate further and in the following summers we dug again and again.

I don't think we caused much real archaeological damage – in fact quite the reverse as in one of those summer digs we found something that turned out to be very important. Roman God-manchester had undergone further improvement and expansion in the third century when a new circuit of town walls was built and a basilica was constructed in the centre of the town. There was no way the Thurley family knew when large chunks of masonry appeared in the bottom of a hole in our garden that we had discovered Godmanchester's basilica, but that is exactly what we had found.

It was a large building, probably used as the town hall. It had massive stone walls and a forecourt with a pillared portico; its floors were probably only gravel but it had a substantial roof of slate and stone. This building must have dominated the small town and seems to have survived a cataclysm that saw the destruction of the *mansio* and baths in the fourth century. It isn't clear what the cataclysm was, but a large hoard of jewellery and coins suggests that whoever was living in the inn had time to hide their goods before the attackers did their worst. Eventually, we don't know when, the basilica too was demolished, its stone probably being used to re-fortify the town walls against attack. We don't know much about the end of Roman Godmanchester. The latest coins are dated AD 293–6, but we know that settlement went on into the fifth century. It is likely, however, that long before then the site of the basilica was lost. Lost in fact for 1,600 years until it reappeared in a late-twentieth-century garden.

Many more lost buildings were to follow the Godmanchester basilica as I left university, embarked on an academic career and eventually was made Curator of the Historic Royal Palaces. There I was able to search for Henry VIII's lost Hampton Court and Edward I's lost Tower of London. At English Heritage, where I now work, I have over 400 buildings in my care, many of which are largely lost too. What I have come to understand over the last fifteen years is that looking for lost buildings is not just a treasure hunt, not only an archaeological search for bricks and mortar. It is a quest for ideas, a search through history to understand what shaped the world we now live in. For great buildings are not simply places in which to live, work and play: they encapsulate something of our way of life, our aspirations and our view of the world. This book is about such buildings. Structures that despite their contemporary fame were lost and never rebuilt, structures that burnt, collapsed or were demolished, but yet are still with us in the way we think about the world. It is about buildings that have made places, that have given birth to ideas, buildings that have had a lasting influence on this country. I have chosen six out of many: an abbey, a country house, a prison, a fortress, a theatre and a royal palace. The choice is not entirely random for these buildings have done more than most to contribute to the quality of our lives: they are structures that have actually shaped our experience of the world. The abbey gave birth to one of the most powerful legends ever, the country house helped trigger an architectural style that still dominates our sense of national identity, the prison transformed our views about punishment, the fortress was at the crux of a struggle for liberty, the theatre saw the birth of modern theatrical practice and the royal palace helped give birth to parliamentary democracy.

People build buildings, live, love and die in buildings, and so the stories of buildings are inextricably mixed up with the lives of people: in the case of these six great buildings, men and women of fame and power. In fact although this book will show how six great buildings helped to shape our world, we must never forget that they were built and moulded by the powerful ambitions and ideas of their creators and owners. The brilliant but dilatory architect James Wyatt and his multimillionaire patron William Beckford, created Fonthill Abbey. Henry II created one of the most impregnable royal castles at Nottingham, which his sons Richard and John fought over. The architect and decorator Robert Adam and the great actor David Garrick came together to create the Theatre Royal, Drury Lane. The penal reformer John Howard and the architect Sir Robert Smirke created Millbank Penitentiary. King James II and his architect Sir Christopher Wren rebuilt White-hall Palace. Glastonbury Abbey, built over a period of almost a thousand years, was seized from its last abbot by King Henry VIII.

These people cannot be readily separated from the buildings they made their own. Each realized, and manipulated, the ability of architecture to change the course of history, to alter the way people live. That is what this unlikely list of characters have in common: they all believed that they could achieve their ends through archi-tecture. Some were building for what we might call moral purposes: Smirke and Howard proposed and designed Millbank Penitentiary because they were appalled by the state of eighteenth-century prisons and wanted to make prisons a force for good, not places of evil and suffering. They believed that if they could design the right building they could reform the criminal mind.

Others built for more selfish reasons: William Beckford, who had been ostracized by society after a homosexual scandal, was certainly building in the hope that his extraordinary house would help him regain his reputation and place in society. David Garrick remodelled the Theatre Royal, Drury Lane because he knew that if he changed the nature of theatregoing by transforming what a theatre was, his business would be a success – it was and he died a very rich man. Nottingham Castle was a much cruder symbol. It was built by the Norman kings as a sign of oppression. It was designed as a base to exercise royal power and authority over the English, and its apparent impregnability was as much for that reason as for any military one. Two of the lost buildings were inspired by a strong ideology. James II's Whitehall Palace was rebuilt as the setting for the type of monarchy that he wanted to create: an absolutist Catholic regime modelled on the monarchy of France. His principal palace had to send out a clear message that his rule was going to be different from what had come before. In Glaston-bury the monks had created an image of their abbey as the oldest and holiest site in England. When it came to surrendering it to Henry VIII for demolition, no wonder the hapless abbot refused. The building stood for so much, he was willing to give his life for it.

Few people would give their lives for a building today. But through history and into our own time people have frequently given their lives for the ideas a building embodies, and that can sometimes mean for the building itself. In July 1789 the workers of the Faubourg St Antoine in Paris stormed the Bastille, the allegedly impregnable royal fortress on the east side of Paris. They broke into the heart of the castle, many being killed by volleys of musket fire, murdered the governor and proceeded to dismantle the building stone by stone. This gesture marked the start of the French Revolution and was a supreme act of defiance against royal authority. The Bastille had become a symbol for royal despotism and cruelty; giving your life in demolishing it was a symbolic blow for freedom. The World Trade Center in New York was, likewise, a symbol of western commercialism and globalization to the terrorists who hijacked two planes and destroyed the twin towers on September 11th. For them the destruction of the towers was a blow for Islamic revolution and against what they saw as the corrosive power and influence of the United States of America.

The World Trade Center was, in its time, a symbol of capitalism – a trademark of New York. In short it was already as much an idea as it was a building. Even with buildings as new as that it is sometimes possible to tell whether it is going to be a structure that will have a lasting influence, for good or ill, or will simply pass away as a footnote in architectural history. In the last years of the twentieth century the Millennium Dome was constructed on Greenwich Peninsula in East London. In a sense it was the successor to the Great Exhibition of 1851 that had created the Crystal Palace in Hyde Park, and the Festival of Britain of 1951 that had created the South Bank and Festival Hall. Like its predecessors, the building was specifically designed to encapsulate the spirit of the age, pushing architecture and engineering to their limits. The Dome succeeded in becoming an icon of its age. Not for the reasons it creators would have wanted, but for its vacuous displays and politically correct messages encapsulating the ideas of a new, modernizing government. After the Scottish decision to accept devolution it was decided, in Whitehall, that the Scots needed their own parliament building. The new building was above all else to be a structure that proclaimed an idea. That was why suggestions to convert existing buildings were rejected. For devolution to work it needed a new building, encapsulating Scottish national pride. We will not know in our lifetime whether this building will be one of ideas. Whether, if it burns down, it will be rebuilt in the same place. Whether, if it is demolished it will be seen to encapsulate a national democracy, like the Houses of Parliament or the Reichstag in Berlin. Yet its purpose, an idea, is likely to live on.

So, buildings, people and ideas fill this book. I hope that they open your eyes to a new way of looking at this country, our history and the way we live, just as they did for me.

Whitehall Palace

The Architecture of Absolutism

On 18 December 1688 Whitehall Palace was the scene of one of the most astonishing events in English history. At eleven o'clock in the morning James II, king of England for just four years, secretly left his bedchamber, passed down the back stairs and stepped out into the cold morning air. Before him was the River Thames and there, moored against the Whitehall jetty, was a small flotilla of boats, including the royal barge. Carrying very little, the 55-year-old monarch boarded. Four or five other barges, already filled with bodyguards, stood by, and as they pulled away James looked back at the building that had been at the centre of his life for the previous twenty-eight years. Only three years before he had begun a major rebuilding of the palace and from his barge he would have seen scaffolding on the half-built queen's private lodgings. The gloomy flotilla pulled away eastwards to take the King to Rochester. There a stage-managed escape enabled him to take a ship to France where he arrived on Christmas Day. James would never see England again.

Dozens of books have been written about James's flight – the Glorious Revolution of 1688 – and historians continue to argue about the causes of his downfall and its consequences. Few focus on Whitehall, the palace from which he left that fateful day. This is partly because the palace, home to monarchs of the Tudor and Stuart dynasty, burnt down almost exactly ten years after James left it. Yet this lost building, once Britain's largest, played a crucial role in the downfall of James II and the establishment of parliamentary democracy in Britain.

Although Whitehall eventually became the largest palace in Europe, and the centre of monarchical power for 168 years, it was

founded by an accident. The seat of English kings since early
Norman times had been at Westminster, on the site later used for
the Houses of Parliament.★ The residential parts of the old Palace
of Westminster were burned down by a terrible fire in 1512 leaving
Henry VIII, who had come to the throne only three years before,
without his principal official residence. Remarkably, Henry did
little about this for seventeen years, apparently being content to
borrow the Archbishop of Canterbury's house across the river at
Lambeth or stay in the City of London instead.

Only in 1529 were the King's residential problems solved, when
he decided to appropriate the Westminster residence of Thomas,
Cardinal Wolsey just a few hundred yards up the road. Wolsey's
house, called York Place, was the London residence of the Archbishop of York. As with Hampton Court, Wolsey had vastly extended this building, making it an attractive and modern residence.
That Henry's covetous eye fell on it is really no surprise.

In the first part of his reign Henry had not been very interested
in architecture. He had been far more excited by hunting and
jousting and other outdoor activities. Building, as with so much
else, he left to his chief councillor, Wolsey. But in the late 1520s
there was a significant change in his attitude to architecture. He
had fallen in love with the intelligent, vivacious and determined
Anne Boleyn. Soon she and Henry were planning their future
together, and in this new buildings loomed large.

In the autumn of 1529, immediately after the fall of Wolsey
(disgraced because he could not procure the King's divorce), Henry
and Anne took a barge down the Thames to pay a visit to York
Place. Henry found the palace more magnificent than he had
remembered it, and Anne was no less impressed. It was perfect
for their immediate purpose. In a royal palace there were always
two suites, one for the king and one for the queen. But as a
churchman, Cardinal Wolsey was not entitled to marry and so at

★ In fact the Houses of Parliament are still officially known as the Palace of
Westminster and briefly become a royal palace again once a year as the royal
standard is raised and the Queen dons her crown at the state opening of
Parliament.

York Place there was simply one suite of rooms for his own use. The existence of only a single suite gave Anne the freedom she needed. There was no space for the King's separated wife, Catherine of Aragon, and so Anne could stay at York Place with the King undisturbed.

That Christmas Anne and Henry, looking to their wedded future, shut themselves away at the royal palace of Greenwich to design themselves a new palace at York Place. James Needham, the King's Master Carpenter, soon to be promoted to Surveyor of the King's Works, must have been summoned to the King's closet. He was almost certainly responsible for designing the new palace to Henry and Anne's specifications. He attended the King with sheets of paper 'of the largest sort' to capture royal ideas and turn them into plans for his workforce. The idea that Henry had was remarkable. His new palace was to be built in two sections, on either side of a busy road. To the west was to be the royal recreation centre, an area of the palace set aside for playing tennis and bowls and for watching cockfights. On the other side of the road were to be the state apartments, incorporating Wolsey's house and centred on a long gallery overlooking beautiful gardens to the south. This long gallery, known as the Privy Gallery, was to contain all the King's own privy (or private) rooms. The two parts of the palace were to be linked by a covered bridge over the road, called the Holbein Gate. The whole complex stretched from present-day Trafalgar Square to the Cenotaph and covered some 23 acres. By Twelfth Night Henry had designed for himself a vast new marital home.

But there was a problem with realizing his plan. York Place was built in the middle of Westminster, a bustling and very prosperous town, in the sixteenth century still separate from the City of London. Shops, houses and inns surrounded the mansion. So Henry sent his surveyors to make a valuation of all the buildings that would be in the way of his new palace. By the spring of 1531 they had done their work and Henry proceeded to purchase their properties from the inhabitants at a cost of £1,130, a very large sum. Almost before the luckless residents could move, the royal demolition

This section of a much larger map of London made in 1560–70
shows Elizabethan Whitehall. At the top (north) is Charing Cross,
now Trafalgar Square; at the bottom Westminster Abbey. The road
marked 'King Street' linked the two and divided Whitehall Palace
in two. The two gates across the road can be seen, with the tennis
courts and cockpit to the left (west) and the residential parts (and
privy garden) to the right (east).

squads had begun their work. A whole suburb of Westminster was demolished to make way for the King's new buildings.

Henry and Anne were obsessed with the building project. By Easter 1532, nearly two and a half years after the plan was first conceived, Anne was publicly acknowledged as the King's mistress and so was able to inspect the progress of work at will. James Needham continually supplied drawings for royal approval, and Henry and Anne improved and refined the design. Queen Anne, as she became in 1533, did not live to see her dream palace completed. She was executed for treason in 1536 with the palace far from finished. Henry, now an obsessive builder, continued the project, which was funded, following the dissolution of the monasteries, by the transfer of Church wealth to the Crown. Henry VIII was suddenly the richest king to ever sit upon the throne; in fact his disposable income increased by 500 per cent. The consequences for Whitehall and the other royal palaces were enormous. From 1536 until the King's death in 1547 the palace was almost permanently a building site. Henry and his subsequent wives had to put up with heavy construction work in close proximity to their lodgings. Although work may have eased off during royal visits, Henry never saw Whitehall free of scaffolding. In the end it was left to Queen Elizabeth I to complete the building that her mother had started fifteen years before.

So what did the completed palace look like? Both contemporary travellers and modern historians have been rude about Whitehall, calling it a jumble or a confusion, and accusing it of lacking any architectural coherence. This, I believe, is to fundamentally misunderstand what was one of the greatest buildings of its age. After the Tudor period the Stuart kings added piecemeal to the palace, spoiling the clarity of the original design and making it hard to appreciate Henry VIII's intentions. But as it stood in the first years of Elizabeth I's reign it was a remarkable and coherent building.

What Henry VIII had done was to set out to build a seat for the dynasty that he wanted to found: it was to be a setting for his court – a court modelled on the chivalric courts of the Middle Ages, and

Although not designed by Holbein, this gateway, which linked the Privy Gallery to the recreation centre, is named after him. Alternating squares of chalk and flint created the chessboard effect. The roundels were of terracotta and some of them can be seen today re-sited on the gatehouses at Hampton Court.

on the legendary court of King Arthur. His intention was to produce a building of magnificence. A building that was set apart by its size, its lavishness and its cost from all others. The style that it was built in I have called 'chivalric eclecticism'. This simply means that by looking back to the castles, tents, heraldry and tournaments of the Middle Ages a new Tudor style was created. It was eclectic in that it drew on ideas from Italy, France, the Middle East and even as far away as India for inspiration. Whitehall Palace was thus a fantasy building, turreted and battlemented, painted, coloured and gilded. The external walls were painted with fantastic beasts, overblown sprigs of acanthus and black and white squares, like a chessboard (see Plate 1). Every pinnacle was crowned with a heraldic beast – a lion or a unicorn or a beast belonging to one of Henry's queens' coats of arms. Many of the beasts held metal flags or vanes painted and gilded to glint in the sun. Approaching the palace by land or by river would have been an amazing experience. Visitors would have felt that they were arriving at the legendary court of King Arthur, the very seat of chivalry.

Inside it was no less magnificent. There were two sets of lodgings, one for the King and another for the Queen. These great suites had ceilings decorated with blue and gold geometrical ribs, friezes of giant coats of arms and badges, while the walls below were covered in the very finest tapestries. There was very little furniture in the outer rooms – the most important objects there were the rich canopies that hung over the royal thrones. The inner, private apartments were much more richly furnished. The walls here were hung not with tapestry but with cloth of gold – that is to say cloth literally woven out of gold thread. The galleries were hung with paintings, often covered in daytime by richly coloured curtains to protect them from the sunlight. The smallest rooms were filled with curiosities: the horns of unicorns, rare minerals, medals, maps, gold and silver work. The royal bedrooms contained beds hung with the most valuable and rare textiles available and spread with the finest linen or silk sheets.

On his death in 1547 an inventory was taken of the contents of all Henry VIII's palaces, including Whitehall. It was a massive task

– Henry was perhaps our most acquisitive monarch – and took eighteen months to complete. The Whitehall inventory demonstrates that it was there that the greatest treasures were kept: items of mother-of-pearl, ebony, ivory, diamonds, jasper, enamel, tortoiseshell, stamped and painted leather, and every type and colour of textile imaginable. There were boxes, chess sets, knives, crossbows, dog collars, medical instruments, combs, pens, sporting equipment – even a string puppet. Whitehall was a cabinet of curiosities and the royal treasure chest.

Henry had amassed palaces almost as greedily: he owned sixty on his death, each with a special function. Whitehall was the most specialized of all, reserved for a particular part of royal life. The first thing to understand is that it was only used in the winter. In the summer months the court went on progress around the country, staying at smaller royal palaces in good hunting areas. Usually the court left Whitehall in the early summer, in late May or early June, and didn't return until October. During that time most of the courtiers would return to their ancestral estates. Many of the royal household, the King's servants, would also go home to their wives and families. In October the royal court would re-enter London and move straight to Whitehall. The nobility and the household would reassemble for the sitting of the law courts and of Parliament, if there was one. Both these were held in the part of Westminster Palace that had survived the 1512 fire, conveniently close to Whitehall. Most of the winter would be spent in the Thames Valley, not only at Whitehall but also at the other great houses on the River Thames: Richmond and Greenwich, both originally built by Henry VII; Hampton Court, also taken from Wolsey; and of course the ancient royal castle of Windsor further west. But Whitehall was the royal base, the King's official residence, like Buckingham Palace today.

So what was a typical day like at Whitehall in Henry's time? Obviously every day was different and as the King grew older his days varied. Yet there are some common strands. Life at Whitehall, and indeed at the other palaces, entirely revolved round the monarch. If you were a courtier your daily mission would be to get as close to the King as possible, as often as possible. Only through Henry could you advance your career. If you were a household servant your role was to do the King's bidding, whatever that might be. So every day there was a tension between the King wanting a degree of privacy – some time alone with his queen, his mistress or his close friends – and the court that continually surged around him wanting a piece, no matter how small, of royal attention.

To resolve this contradiction English monarchs had developed a code of conduct, an etiquette, which had to be followed by every-one at court. This code, a written set of household regulations, set out what one was permitted to do, when one was allowed to do it, and how one should effect it. Henry's Lord Chamberlain was in charge of the regulations and anyone who stepped outside them was punished. There were two things anyone working at court had to remember: the first was their rank and role – what their duties were and how to undertake them; and the second was where they were allowed to go. The palace was divided into three strictly policed zones. The outer rooms, which were the most public ones, were where almost anyone well dressed could go. The inner private rooms (called the privy lodgings) were only open to a limited number of household servants and courtiers, and the most private rooms (called the secret places) were only for the King and one or two named individuals. The regulations set out who was allowed into each zone and what their roles were within it. To the modern mind this sounds unnecessarily complicated, but in reality it was the only way that the court could function. Because Henry was the sole source of power, advancement and wealth, he was potentially on duty twenty-four hours a day. The household regulations thus protected the King and created a system that allowed the maximum number of people to have access to him.

There was another important dimension to the system. A royal palace was not just a residence: it was a machine for governing. Whitehall, above all other residences, was the centre of government and state ceremonial and had a special status as the monarch's princi-pal residence – combining, in modern terms, the functions of Buck-ingham Palace, 10 Downing Street and most of the government offices along Whitehall. Beneath the King's lodgings on the ground floor were the lodgings of the principal men at court – the secretaries of state, the Archbishop of Canterbury and the Lord Chancellor. Just off the Privy Gallery, opposite the door to the King's bed-chamber, was the Council Chamber – the room in which what we would call the Cabinet (then the Privy Council) met. This amazingly close proximity is what still exists to a lesser extent at Downing Street today: all the key people in government living and working in a single building, their private, public and governmental lives hopelessly mixed up.

If we take a look at the way Henry VIII lived at Whitehall it becomes apparent that this entanglement of public and private, of governance and daily life, dominated his life. At dawn he would get up and go into the privy chamber adjoining his bedchamber where his closest servants would dress and shave him in private. His clothes would be brought up from the royal wardrobe, situated beneath his lodgings on the ground floor. Meanwhile the rest of the court would be waking all over the palace: courtiers in their own lodgings, tucked into the maze of courtyards and passages; and 250 servants in their lodgings on the north side, in an area known as Scotland Yard. While the King was prepared for his day the household servants would clean the outer rooms of the palace, sweep the courts and light the kitchen fires. Henry would take his breakfast in the privy lodgings, it having been prepared in his own privy kitchen. The great kitchen that prepared food for everyone else was an enormous, cumbersome section of the household that specialized in mass catering. The King needed his food in his own lodgings, cooked to his own taste and delivered when he wanted it. Henry thus had his own chef – a Frenchman called Pierre.

Once dressed Henry would go to his private chapel to hear Mass. On every weekday (that was not a Church feast) Henry would kneel in the closet next to his privy chamber for his daily devotion. Next to the closet was a small chapel divided from the King's kneeling place by a screen with a latticework window. Through this, each morning, the King would hear a royal chaplain celebrate

Mass. His closet was lavishly decorated with precious hangings and carpets and probably a valuable crucifix and jewelled missal. On Sundays and the great Church feasts such as Easter and Christmas the King would go to the main palace chapel. At Whitehall this was part of the palace that Cardinal Wolsey had built. It would have been much like an Oxford or Cambridge college chapel is today, but with an upper gallery from which the King would view the service. The chapel at Hampton Court still retains this arrangement and looks much as Henry would have known it. The service, although the excuse, was not the most important part of the King's attendance at chapel. Visiting the chapel gave Henry the chance to process from his privy lodgings through the great outer state rooms of Whitehall to the chapel. As he did so the route would not only be lined by his bodyguards and household servants, but by the entire court and many other spectators. This was one of the great spectacles of the court and the best chance to see the King if you were not one of his close servants.

For the rest of the day until dinner time Henry had a number of choices as to what he could do. One choice was recreation. Half of Whitehall was a recreation centre containing four tennis courts, a bowling alley and a cockpit. Rather surprisingly Henry VII, usually considered to be a dour and staid monarch, had taken up tennis with gusto at the age of thirty-seven and subsequently ensured that Prince Henry and his siblings were all taught the game. When Henry VIII came to the throne in 1509 he was already an accomplished tennis player, although he much preferred the more aggressive and energetic sports of jousting and hunting. But as Whitehall rose, Henry and Anne Boleyn turned to the gentler and more middle-aged sport of real tennis. Real tennis, still played today, was an early version of modern lawn tennis, but much more complicated, slower, and played on an elaborate court. There were four courts at Whitehall, two indoors and two outdoors. Henry played on all of them. The courts were designed with galleries from which courtiers could watch the game and bet on the outcome. Henry was a genuinely good player and often (but by no means always) won. On his death in 1547 seven tennis rackets were found in his study at Greenwich and a black velvet tennis coat and slippers, a sort of Tudor tracksuit and trainers, were in his wardrobe. When the King was not playing the courts were rented by courtiers. At two shillings and sixpence a day it was quite an expensive recreation, quite beyond the means of ordinary people.

The bowling alley was 160 feet long and about 20 feet wide. The game played in it was a cross between tenpin bowling and bowls, the aim of it being to get your ball as close to the jack at the other end as possible. Just like the tennis matches, the outcome of the game was the subject of wagers. The alley was a modest, low building, but much more spectacular was the cockpit. This extraordinary structure was the architectural centrepiece of the recreation centre. It contained a circular arena with a special seat for the King. In the middle was a low, round platform on to which two cocks were placed. Each would have spurs strapped to its legs and a little hood over its head. Yet again bets were laid, and the cock that survived the mortal combat won. Prize cocks were highly valued and Henry's best ones were kept in special coops under the stage.

On the east side of the palace, to the south of the Privy Gallery, lay the palace gardens. The focus of a royal garden in the 1530s and 40s was very different from a garden of today. It served two distinct purposes: it was designed to be seen by indoor spectators from the upper galleries of the palace, and also to be walked in by invited courtiers. From the palace windows it looked like a giant chessboard divided into large squares of coloured gravel. The squares were divided up by low shin-rails painted green and white – the Tudor colours (see Plate 1). At the intersection of the squares were tall green-and-white posts topped with heraldic beasts. The garden was an exercise in heraldry, just like the palace. But when courtiers took a walk in the garden – and only the privileged were allowed to do so – it was a very different experience. The edges of the squares were planted with aromatic herbs and little flowers that made a walk on a warm evening a heady experience. At the southern end of the garden was a banqueting house where the King, Queen and their guests might go after dinner to eat sweetmeats. Beyond that was a square of grass laid out for bowling.

If the King tired of the sports provided in the recreation centre, or walking in his garden, he could go hunting. At the same time that Henry purchased most of northern Westminster for demolition he bought a huge amount of land on the west side to form a chain of hunting parks. Today we call these St James's Park, Green Park, Hyde Park and Regent's Park, but then they were royal hunting grounds. Henry could ride on his own land from Whitehall as far west as Kensington and as far north as St John's Wood. Of these, St James's Park was the closest and most important. It was walled round and contained ponds stocked with fish and waterfowl, as well as deer, rabbits and pheasants. Many of these were ornamental, but sometimes the King would shoot or fish in the park.

It would be quite wrong to portray Whitehall as simply a palace for pleasure, because in many respects it was the opposite of that. The outlying palaces of Greenwich and Hampton Court were much more closely devoted to pleasure, while Whitehall was always the working palace. Many days Henry would have Council meetings, or receive ambassadors seated on his throne in the state apartments. He would receive petitions or delegations and create knights in public ceremonies. This was the purpose of Whitehall, and as soon as work would allow, Henry and the court would move on to one of the Thames-side palaces in the country. In many ways the recreation centre, the garden and the parks were for the courtiers who would have to wait for the King to finish state business before turning his attention to pleasure.

In the late afternoon Henry would have his principal meal of the day. It would be served to him in his privy chamber, where he sat alone under a canopy. Waiting upon him would be some of the greatest and most important lords in the land. After dinner Henry might visit the Queen's apartments, sited on the riverfront. Here the household regulations did not apply and the atmosphere was less formal. The King might play the harpsichord, dance, listen to music, or read poetry. At the end of the day Henry would retire to his bedchamber, that is unless he had arranged to sleep with the

Queen. In that case he would stay in the Queen's bedchamber, where they could make love uninterrupted by the royal officials who slept in and around the King's bedroom.

This mode of life established by Henry VIII continued in all its essentials right up to the reign of Charles II. Individual monarchs made adjustments, and individual regulations were refined and altered. The precise boundaries of the zones in the palace changed over the years. Yet the basic truth was that Charles II in the 1660s lived in a very similar way to Henry VIII in the 1540s. Much the same could be said of the palace itself. Although new buildings had been added; although old buildings had been altered and improved; although monarchs had extended their private quarters and built new rooms for their favourites or mistresses, the palace of 1660 was broadly the palace that Henry VIII left on his death. The principal exception was the construction, by James I, of the Banqueting House, the only substantial part of the palace to survive today. This vast stone building, that rose next to the Holbein Gate, dwarfed the maze of brick structures that surrounded it. Designed by Inigo Jones and completed by 1622, it was intended by James I to be the ceremonial hub of the palace, replacing Henry VIII's Great Hall. Charles I adorned it with the remarkable painted ceiling by Peter Paul Rubens for which it is now famous, and in 1649 lost his life on a scaffold outside it at the hands of a rebellious Parliament.

In 1660 Charles II and his brother James (later James II) returned to Whitehall in triumph. Many times over the previous fifteen or so years as they had wandered round northern Europe the two brothers had felt that their cause was lost. Cromwell's execution of their father, Charles I, outside the Banqueting House and the establishment of the republican Commonwealth must have seemed fairly permanent. Only with hindsight do we see the Cromwellian period as an interlude.

Charles had been in exile in Paris while Louis XIV was rebuilding his principal residence of the Louvre. This was the greatest architectural enterprise in northern Europe, undertaken by the man who would become Europe's most powerful and fashionable ruler, and

A Continental print depicting the execution of Charles I outside the Banqueting House on 30 January 1649. James I built the Banqueting House in the 1620s as a glorification of his reign and his dynasty. The execution of his son Charles outside it reinforced the building's iconic status for the Stuart monarchs.

it made a big impact upon Charles. He returned to Whitehall in 1660 with his mind full of French architecture, French design and French fashions. What he found on the banks of the Thames must have been profoundly depressing to him. Despite the improvements made by his father and grandfather, Whitehall was still the palace of Henry VIII. Worse still it was semi-derelict. Despite the fact that Cromwell had lived there, his troops had treated it badly. Many rooms had been divided up for offices, and parts had been used as a barracks or even as a prison. Despite the efforts of the architect John Webb to prepare it for Charles's reception it must have looked very old fashioned and unloved.

In the first years after the Restoration, despite a widespread feeling that Charles was going to rebuild the palace, little happened, mainly because the political and economic conditions were not right. On 28 October 1664, however, the diarist John Evelyn recorded a remarkable occasion. He was 'casually in the Privy Gallery at White-hall' speaking to the King, who asked whether Evelyn had a crayon and paper. Evelyn 'presented him with both and then laying it on the window stoole, he with his owne hands, designed to me the plot for the future building of Whitehall, together with the Roomes of state & other particulars'. Sadly the King's sketch does not survive, and so we cannot know what it was that he drew for Evelyn, but we do know that during that autumn Christopher Wren was already helping Charles to design a new palace at Whitehall. As a professor of astronomy and a founding member of the Royal Society, Wren had first come to the notice of Charles II through the King's love of scientific experiments and astronomy. Wren had an obvious aptitude for building, and this led, as early as 1661, to an offer from the King for Wren to become the next surveyor of the royal building works. The fact that Wren was working on a major scheme for rebuilding Whitehall with the King in the autumn of 1664 is astonishing for a man who had designed little and built even less. It was partly because of this that in January 1665 Charles II sent him to Paris to see Louis XIV's palace of the Louvre and to meet the French royal architect Mansard and the famous Italian architect and sculptor Gian Lorenzo Bernini. This trip was to be one of the most important influences on Wren's life and architecture, and had important consequences for Whitehall.

In Paris Wren went to the Louvre building site every day and closely watched not only the craftsmen at work, but their engineering methods and construction techniques. He also managed to grab an interview with Bernini himself and snatch a glimpse at his drawings. Leaving Paris, he then went on a tour of all the most modern houses and palaces in the vicinity and systematically bought every architectural book and print he could lay his hands on. On his return to London Wren's imagination was fired with everything he had seen, and books and notes weighted down his baggage. He must have briefed Charles on the developing plans for the Louvre and shown him his prints and sketches. The court was soon full of rumours that work would start on the rebuilding of Whitehall at any moment, but before Wren could put pen to paper the monarchy was overwhelmed by a disaster. The Great Fire of London of 1666 put paid to any idea of rebuilding Whitehall. Not only would it have been an act of monumental insensitivity to start rebuilding with the city in ruins; it has to be doubted whether the craftsmen, materials or money would have been available. Not to mention the fact that Wren now was responsible for overseeing the rebuilding of St Paul's Cathedral and fifty-one City parish churches. Charles had to shelve his thoughts of a new Whitehall and make do with some much lesser temporary improvements.

Wren's notable success in rebuilding the City and his increasing royal favour were to lead to his appointment in 1669 as Surveyor of the King's Works, whereupon he finally assumed official responsibility for the redesign of Whitehall. To get things started, Wren commissioned a comprehensive survey of the palace from the mathematical instrument maker and surveyor Ralph Greatorex, who had just completed a survey of the Royal Arsenal at Woolwich. This triggered a spate of speculation about the palace's future. The survey, completed in 1670, is the single most important document for the study of the palace. First, it is a detailed and very accurate record of the palace as it stood, an essential prerequisite to the process of redesign and reconstruction. Second, it records exactly who had lodgings and where. The palace had more than 1,500 rooms to lodge courtiers and by 1670 these had been granted out to the 100 or so individuals identified on the plan and no doubt to more not shown. The survey demonstrates that Whitehall was not just a building: it was a teeming village of more than 1,000 inhabitants. If the palace was to be rebuilt, these people would have to be consulted, moved and rehoused. Yet, despite this survey, continued financial difficulties throughout the 1670s meant that it is unlikely that Wren even began the design work necessary for rebuilding Whitehall. In fact Charles II failed to rebuild the

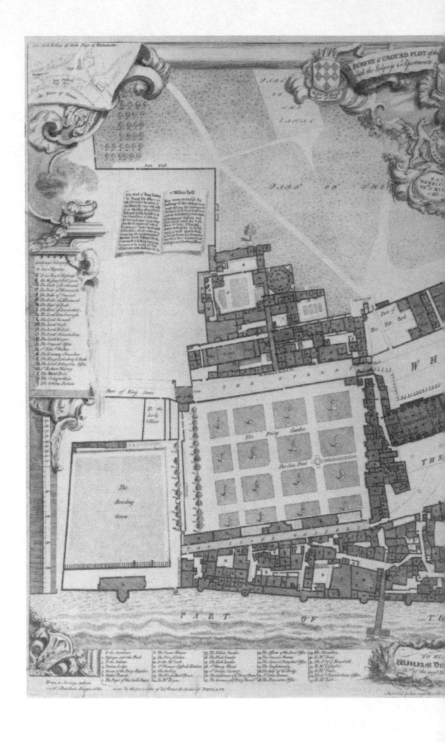

This is a print made in about 1747 of Greatorex's 1670 survey of the palace of Whitehall. It shows the palace at its greatest extent and contains a key listing its principal occupants.

crumbling Tudor palace of Whitehall and give the English monarchy its Louvre.

His brother James II, who came to the throne in 1685, was more
determined. It seems certain that even before Charles was dead,
James was working on ideas for the reconstruction of Whitehall in
a style that would fit his future monarchy. James was very different
from his brother, who had skilfully managed to rehabilitate the
monarchy despite war, economic crisis and religious discord. James
strongly believed that his right to rule as king was a gift and a
commission directly from God. In other words, that he ruled by
divine right. Unlike his brother, who had also believed this, he
wanted to model his rule on the authoritarian rule of Louis XIV of
France and had little time for the notion of Parliament. He also
wanted to re-establish Britain as a Catholic nation safely in the fold
of Rome. Catholic absolutist monarchy in France was being played
out against the backdrop of the absolutist architecture of Versailles,
and James wanted a palace at Whitehall that spoke of his determination to rule autocratically. Two things were therefore necessary:
to rebuild the higgledy-piggledy Privy Gallery that had been the
core of the palace since Henry VIII's time, and give it a dignity and
authority that it lacked; and to build a major Roman Catholic
chapel for himself and his queen, Mary of Modena. His instructions
to Sir Christopher Wren were simple. He asked him to design a
suite of new apartments for the Queen facing the privy garden, to
give the south front of the palace a modern appearance. In this
range there would also be a new Council Chamber, from which
he would rule, and a new chapel, ostensibly the Queen's but in
reality a Catholic chapel in the heart of the palace where he could
attend Mass.

This was a reckless idea. The English Civil War had been, as
much as anything else, a war of religion. Charles I had become
tainted by his marriage to Catholic Henrietta Maria and his toler-
ation of her Catholic chapels. Charles I's execution on a scaffold
outside the Banqueting House at Whitehall had been not only a
blow against the monarchy, but against the sort of High Church
religion that was practised in Charles's court. In 1660 Charles II

knew that in returning to the throne the single most important thing he had to achieve was the re-establishment of a Protestant Church of England supported by a Protestant monarch as head of the Church. Even for a king as single-minded as Charles this proved difficult. Londoners were suspicious of his Portuguese Catholic wife, Catherine of Braganza; they were suspicious of his Catholic mother, Henrietta Maria; they were suspicious of his French Catholic mistress, Louise de Keroualle; and of his relationship with Louis XIV. Most of all they were suspicious of his brother James, who had done little to convince anyone that he was not actually a Catholic himself.

It is hard today to understand the anti-Catholic paranoia of London in the 1670s and 80s. The closest modern parallel is the cold war, when the whole nation was suspicious of Communists and the threat they posed to national peace and security. Londoners of the 1670s and 80s genuinely believed that there were Catholics in hiding who were ready to come out and murder English Protestants in their beds, and a French army poised to conquer England and impose a totalitarian Catholic regime. Unfortunately for Charles, James's Catholic leanings turned into an outright conversion to Catholicism in 1669. Soon this was public and the Whigs in Parliament attempted to make it impossible, by law, for James to become king. Historians call the terrible political turmoil this caused the Exclusion Crisis. It was a crisis that Charles II resisted. Thus when he suddenly died in 1685 James, unopposed, became the first Catholic monarch since Henry VIII to sit on the throne of England.

Within only three months of Charles II's death, plans for the new queen's apartments had been agreed, and in May 1685 Wren submitted his estimate for the work. In essence what was being proposed was a new queen's apartment, with rooms above for her ladies and servants, on the site of the old Privy Gallery. At the west end, by the Holbein Gate, would be the new Roman Catholic chapel. On the north side of the new range, behind the Banqueting House, a new stair would provide access to a new Privy Gallery and Council Chamber, and the Banqueting House. On the ground

Plan of Whitehall Palace during the reign of James II. By the 1680s most of the west-side recreation centre had been converted into lodgings for members of the court and royal family. The regularity of James's new south range can be compared to the confusion of the rest of the ground plan.

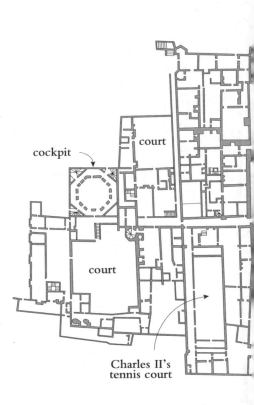

cockpit

court

court

Charles II's
tennis court

King Street
Gate

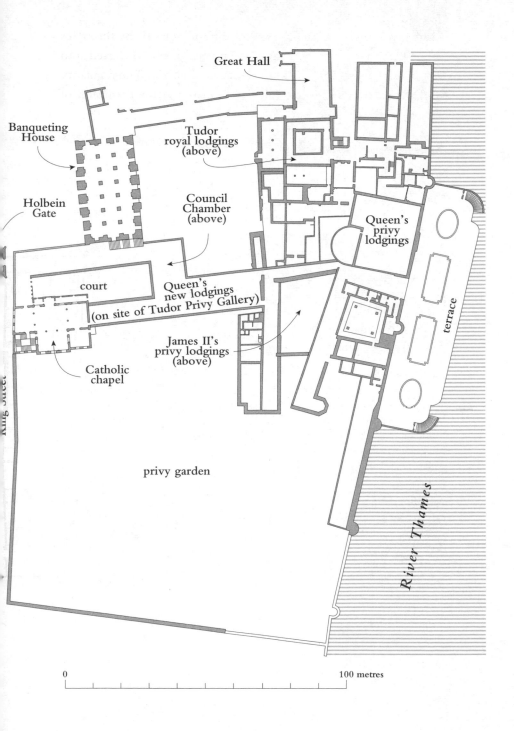

Great Hall

Banqueting
House

Tudor
royal lodgings
(above)

Holbein
Gate

Council
Chamber
(above)

Queen's
privy
lodgings

court

Queen's
new lodgings
(on site of Tudor Privy Gallery)

James II's
privy lodgings
(above)

Catholic
chapel

terrace

privy garden

King Street

River Thames

0   100 metres

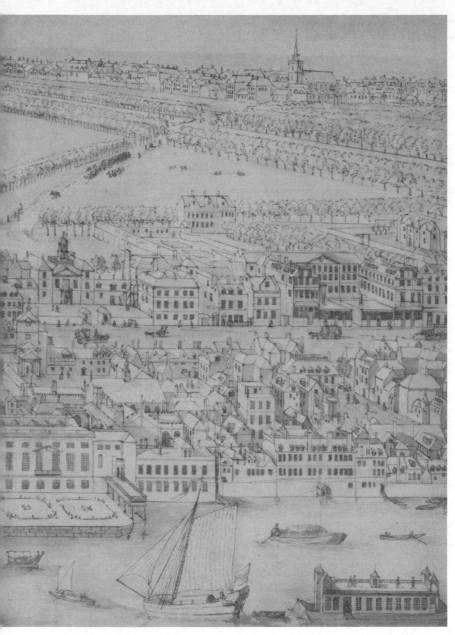

This view of 1695–7 by the Dutch topographical artist Leonard Knyff shows, with clarity, the layout of James's new buildings: the range facing the privy garden, terminating in the chapel; the location of a small court behind it; the staircase at the south end of the Banqueting House, and the new Council Chamber. The southern end of the site has been cleared after the fire of 1691.

floor all the offices of state which were formerly under the Privy Gallery, including the Treasury offices, were to be rebuilt. Work was rapid and John Evelyn saw the Queen's bed in her new apartments in January 1687. Leonard Knyff's bird's-eye view of the palace of circa 1695–7 shows the new lodgings. It also shows that Wren cleverly blended the new buildings with the Banqueting House in an attempt to bring harmony to the exterior of Whitehall again.

The new chapel was started in May 1685, just months after the death of Charles. It was to be the greatest royal ecclesiastical commission since the completion of Henry VII's chapel at Westminster Abbey. The designer was Sir Christopher Wren, whose rebuilding of St Paul's Cathedral and the City churches had created an Anglican style of church architecture. This building was a substantial challenge for him. James wanted it to be suitable for the most magnificent ceremonies of the Roman Catholic Church, to be conducted by Jesuit priests. Wren would have had very little idea of how to build a church suitable for this type of liturgy. True, he had seen Jesuit churches when he visited Paris, but this was now twenty years ago. So he turned to the only Catholic chapels still in existence in England: the queen's chapels at St James's Palace and Somerset House. These two chapels had been built by Inigo Jones in the 1620s for Charles I's Catholic wife and had been used by both Henrietta Maria and Catherine of Braganza. The chapel at St James's survives today and can be visited on Sundays for services. It is a relatively plain rectangular box with a balcony (or pew) at one end for the monarch. The ceiling is vaulted and magnificent, but plain white and unpainted. Wren's design for the new chapel at Whitehall followed the plan of these two buildings: a plain rectangle with a vaulted ceiling and an altarpiece at the east end. In Protestant services, the sermon, prayer and biblical readings – and thus a prominent pulpit – are of great importance, but Catholic worship concentrates on the celebration of Communion. In this the altarpiece is the architectural focus, as the backdrop to the elevation of the consecrated bread, and of its permanent receptacle, the tabernacle. The altarpiece is therefore the principal vehicle for decoration in a Catholic church. Wren, of course, had little experience of designing such a thing. He had seen Jesuit churches with vigorous Counter-Reformation altarpieces in Paris and may have even brought engravings of them back to England in his parcel of books. However it is more likely that James himself had acquired engravings of the very latest Catholic church architecture and that either he or the Queen gave Wren engravings to copy.

James was in a tearing hurry. Grinling Gibbons and Arnold Quellin, the greatest carvers of their day, were given the £1,800 contract to build the great altarpiece in the new chapel. It was to be 39 foot, 6 inches high and span the entire 33 foot width of the chapel's east end. Their contract specified that the altar should be finished by 25 September 1686 or else the craftsmen had to forfeit £100 of their fee. This was an incredible task, and Gibbons and Quellin had to employ almost fifty carvers, joiners, painters, stone-masons and polishers to assist them. The altarpiece was made of white marble, three storeys high, topped with two life-size kneeling marble angels. The Catholic Italian artist Benedetto Gennario, who had worked at the English court since 1674, supplied three paintings for the chapel. His main work at the court of Charles II had been producing Catholic images for the Queen and the Duke of York, and on James's accession he suddenly had a Catholic monarch as his patron. His masterpiece was to be an Annunciation painted for the space over the main altar, measuring 7 feet by 8 feet. Another Catholic painter, Antonio Verrio, painted the chapel ceiling, which depicted the Assumption of the Blessed Virgin.

Grinling Gibbons was also contracted to provide a wooden pulpit carved with figures of the four Evangelists, a picture frame for Gennario's altarpiece and a marble holy water pot. Opposite the altar was the royal pew, or tribune, as it was called. In this balcony (similar to a box at the theatre) a canopy of nine carved and gilded cherubs and a gilded crown and sceptre were suspended over the King and Queen's thrones.

The new chapel was used for the first time on Christmas Eve 1686. The King and Queen sat in regal splendour in their new

James II's altarpiece was removed from his Roman Catholic chapel before Whitehall burnt in 1698. It was later given to Westminster Abbey by Queen Anne. There it was re-erected with some small modifications. This engraving made in 1808 shows the altarpiece at Westminster much as James II would have known it.

pew and listened to an Italian choir singing Mass while a Roman Catholic bishop presided in his mitre and rich cope. There were also ten Jesuit priests with rich vestments swinging censers, filling the chapel with incense. John Evelyn was shocked at what he saw. 'I could not have believed that I should ever have seen such things in the King of England's palace,' he wrote in his diary.

Despite the magnificence of the midnight Mass and the shock it caused James's Protestant subjects, the chapel was deemed a failure. Wren's design was not really suitable for either Roman Catholic worship or the degree of ceremony required by the King and Queen. On 10 April 1687 Wren received instructions to alter and enlarge it. He was asked to build a processional staircase linking the royal pew with the chapel below so that the King and Queen could process to the altar rail and take Communion in public. He was also instructed to build a side chapel for a subsidiary altar, and above it a new organ loft.

While the chapel was architecturally the most important part of James's buildings at Whitehall, there were also magnificent new rooms for the Queen, with ceilings painted by Verrio and painted and gilded walls. There was also the new Council Chamber, with rooms nearby for the royal clerks and a waiting room for people summoned to appear before the Privy Council. The whole new range must have looked something like the south front of Kensington Palace does today. It was brick with a stone-clad basement and stone dressings around important architectural features. No one could really pretend that this was the architecture of absolutism, even though it cost James the enormous sum of £35,343. What James built was very English and was essentially very modest. But that didn't really matter. The speed at which the buildings were constructed and the knowledge that at the heart of the new range was an enormous Roman Catholic chapel was enough to incense Londoners.

The royal Catholic chapels at Somerset House and St James's Palace had been at the heart of violent opposition to Charles I in the 1640s. The moment Charles had left London and raised his standard against Parliament at Nottingham in 1642 the chapels were targets for destruction. The Somerset House chapel was stripped of its fittings and the priceless altarpiece by Rubens was stabbed by pikes and tossed into the Thames. During the Commonwealth Cromwell had the Somerset House chapel used as a Protestant preaching house. The chapel at St James's was turned into a library.

At the Restoration Charles II had battled for the right of his queen, Catherine of Braganza, to have her own Catholic chapel. Again and again he was petitioned for the Queen's chapels to be closed, and eventually he had to confine Catherine to a single chapel at St James's and deny her the use of the chapel at Somerset House. James thus cannot have been unaware either of the provocation that Catholic chapels caused or of the storm that building a very large one at Whitehall must provoke. Yet he went ahead.

In the events leading up to his flight in December 1688 the Whitehall chapel played its part. The first popular riot of James's reign was in April 1686, when a mob provoked by the opening of a Catholic chapel in Lime Street, in the City, stormed a service and dragged one Catholic worshipper through the gutter. Much worse was the general lawlessness of the autumn of 1688, when a whole series of Catholic chapels across London were attacked and the interiors smashed up. James decided that this could not be tolerated and announced the closure of all Catholic chapels except – and this is the important point – his own and those used by foreign ambassadors. These remaining chapels were given a heavy guard. James's new chapel shone out like a beacon to Londoners as the most visible symbol of James's contempt for not only the Church of England, but the feelings of true Englishmen. By the autumn of 1688 James's rule was almost untenable. He had succeeded in alienating almost everyone whose support he needed to stay in power.

For a long time people had known that there was an alternative to James. The Dutch prince of Orange, William, had as his mother Mary, one of Charles I's daughters, and had married James II's daughter from his first marriage with (Protestant) Anne Hyde. William of Orange and his wife Princess Mary thus had a double claim to the English throne and, importantly, they were Protestants. William and Mary were king and queen in waiting, the natural heirs on the death of James. But on 10 June 1688 James's queen gave birth to a healthy son at St James's Palace. Despite the best efforts of his detractors to prove that the child was a changeling smuggled into the palace, it was clear that there was a Catholic heir and that William's previously sparkling claim had suddenly become tarnished. On both side of the English Channel moves were afoot to remove James from the throne.

By September 1688 it was public knowledge that William of Orange was preparing an army ready for invasion. The corridors of Whitehall were filled with rumour and a palpable sense of unease. James was beside himself with anxiety and sent orders to mobilize the Army. A royal proclamation was issued stating that it was a pretence that he had threatened the 'liberties, property and religion' of the English and that these lies were being used as a cover to facilitate the conquest of England by the Dutch. In a state of panic James began to systematically overturn all the pro-Catholic actions that he had introduced since his accession. But it was not enough. Everyone knew that the moment the threat of invasion subsided, or the day William of Orange was beaten, James would simply reinstate the unpopular measures. On 28 September the King and Queen retreated to the new Whitehall chapel where they began a forty-hour service of continuous prayer for divine assistance

Even James knew that prayer was not going to be enough and by mid October his army was positioned along the south and east coast and his navy was ready to sail. All they awaited was a favourable wind for William to leave Holland. On top of the Banqueting House, in the heart of Whitehall, the king's blacksmiths laboured to erect a huge weather vane. It is still there on the north side, easily visible from the street. On 1 November 1688 the gilded vane flipped eastwards, signalling that William's fleet was on the way. It landed four days later, on 5 November, at Torbay.

James moved to Salisbury, where a large part of his army lay in wait for the invaders. It was not a happy visit. Parts of the Army were deserting to join William's forces and the stress caused James to have a two-day-long nosebleed that prevented him from travelling. He decided to retreat to the Thames Valley and create a strong defensive line around London. But by the time he returned to Whitehall he found that the drizzle of defections had turned into a deluge. Worse, amongst the defectors were some of his closest and oldest friends, and some of the most important men of the court. The most crushing news was that his daughter Anne (later Queen Anne) had left Whitehall with the Bishop of London and was on her way to join William of Orange's camp. Already there, waiting for her, was her husband, George of Denmark.

Even James now realized that his reign was untenable. Both his daughters, both his sons-in-law, and his closest and oldest friends were now all against him. The court had shrunk to a tiny group of Catholic advisors and a few minor Italian diplomats. He heard that Dover Castle, his obvious escape route to the Continent, had gone over to William. It would be surprising if James, sitting in Whitehall on the night of 9 December, did not think of the execution of his father, not thirty yards from where he slept. Over a tense and unhappy supper James and his wife, Mary of Modena, agreed to flee, probably as a temporary measure to allow things to calm down – they thought they would return when it was proved that William could not win the support of the people.

At two o'clock in the morning on 10 December the Queen, disguised as an Italian laundress, left Whitehall with the Prince of Wales, two nurses and a single attendant. She was smuggled to Gravesend in a coach, where she embarked for France. The King, meanwhile, was struggling with his own conscience: should he stay or should he abandon his duty and go? In the early hours of 11 December, less than twenty-four hours after the Queen, James boarded a carriage in the inner court at Whitehall. It took him to the horse ferry at Lambeth, where he crossed the river. In his luggage he had the Great Seal of England, the instrument by which Parliament was called. In the wintry darkness the heavy metal mould, the symbol of royal authority, was slipped into the river. Although few knew that he had thrown the Seal away, the very action of his abandoning the throne at a time of national crisis was to count against him. Kings were expected to rule, and if they could not a council of regency should be established. James had simply dropped the reins of power.

Court etiquette restricted access into the King's bedchamber and so it was not until the middle of the next morning that it became

A romanticized seventeenth-century print showing the flight of
James II from Whitehall in December 1688.

clear that he had fled. His attempt to escape was a disaster. The
whole of the Thames Estuary and most of Kent was full of parties
of armed peasants and townsmen looking for papists, and so it was
not long before a rough band apprehended the King's party and
James found himself in captivity. His rough cloak, short wig and a
patch on the side of his face concealed his identity from his captors.
He was stripped, searched and his crucifix confiscated. When he
arrived at Faversham he was recognized as the king and, eventually,
treated as such.

William of Orange was by now at Windsor Castle, and James
believed that, even at this late stage, he could strike a deal with his
son-in-law that would heal the wounds and secure his throne. To
start negotiations he returned to Whitehall, being welcomed on his
arrival in London by cheering crowds and celebratory bonfires. In
his absence there had been terrifying riots – the houses of known

Catholics had been ransacked and Catholic chapels burnt. Londoners, seeing their king, hoped that he had done a deal with William and that peace would return. Everyone, William and James included, wanted to avoid bloodshed and chaos. That night, 17 December, was surreal. With William at Syon House on the outskirts of London, and James buoyed by his reception, Whitehall almost returned to normal. The King regally summoned his Privy Council to the new Council Chamber and welcomed his Catholic advisors back to his apartments. At midnight he ostentatiously heard Mass in the chapel.

In the middle of the following night the King was woken in his bedchamber by the Earl of Middleton, who was sleeping at the foot of the King's bed. William had stationed Dutch guards round Whitehall and the King's own grenadiers had defected to the Prince. James capitulated and agreed to leave Whitehall. At eleven the next morning a small flotilla of barges pulled up at the steps of Whitehall and rowed England's rightful king away to Rochester from where, on Christmas Eve, he left for France. Only five hours later Prince William of Orange rode into London and established himself at St James's Palace. The Glorious, and bloodless, Revolution had been effected.

The coming of William and Mary changed the nature of government in England for ever. They came to rule at the invitation of Parliament, and ruled the people by their consent, not by divine right. James's dream of royal autocratic rule could now never come to pass. Nor could his dream of a Roman Catholic monarchy: Parliament made it illegal for a Roman Catholic to sit on the British throne.

After their coronation William III and Mary II moved into Whitehall. The building that greeted them was far from their liking. They had been used to the small, neat, well-ordered palaces of the Netherlands, set in the clean air of the Dutch countryside. Whitehall was a monster: massive, crowded, dirty, low-lying, and in the middle of the largest city in Europe. The damp of the river and the coal smoke of the city aggravated King William's asthma, and he and Mary decided to move immediately to Hampton Court. Yet they could not ignore Whitehall – it was the seat of power and the location of all the key government offices. William must have looked at his father-in-law's new buildings with interest. While the new apartments may have seemed magnificent enough, the Catholic chapel was repellent to him. Orders were given to transform it into a library. The great marble altarpiece was carefully dismantled and put in store. The two Catholic painters who had adorned the walls of the room left court: Gennario followed James into exile; Verrio left London for the provinces.

William and Mary never really liked Whitehall. In the first weeks of their reign Sir Christopher Wren was ordered to build them a new palace at Kensington. In future William and Mary would reside here and travel the short distance across the park to Whitehall when required. For the first time since Henry VIII the link between residence at Whitehall and the government of the country was broken. While William and Mary's attention was focused on Kensington and their project to rebuild Hampton Court, disaster struck at Whitehall. On 9 April 1691 a maid working for the Duke of Gloucester (Anne's son, and William and Mary's nephew) accidentally ignited a bunch of candles that set fire to the Duke's lodging in the south-east corner of the palace. The fire quickly gripped the oldest and most densely packed part of the palace. As the residents of the lodgings rapidly cleared out their possessions, the palace firefighters set to work dousing the flames. The lodgings were a long way from the royal apartments, but as the firefighters lost control of the blaze it was decided to create a firebreak by blowing up part of the building to prevent the fire reaching the main palace. The plan worked, and after five hours the crisis was over. William and Mary showed little concern. They had thought the palace too big anyway, and the destruction of the southern part provided the opportunity to tidy up and improve the rambling building.

The 1691 fire left all Charles II's and James II's new work unscathed. Knyff's view shows the southern part of the palace site, by the waterside, clear of buildings. The fire had in fact removed the largest surviving residential parts of the Tudor palace and created an even greater sense of order to the remaining buildings. But while the fire of 1691 was limited in its extent and consequences, the conflagration of 4 January 1698 effectively destroyed the entire residential part of the palace. This fire started in the top floor of the lodgings of Colonel Stanley, where a Dutch maidservant was drying linen sheets. It was not uncommon to light a charcoal brazier for this purpose, or even to hang sheets over one, but it was forbidden to leave them unattended. In the temporary absence of the maid the sheets ignited and set fire to the hangings, to Stanley's bed, and then to his whole lodging. Despite the rebuilding of James II's time, Whitehall was still largely a timber building. The roof voids across the whole site interconnected and so it was easy for the flames to travel from building to building. Before long flames were rising from the whole southern part of the palace.

As soon as the fire was noticed, palace staff were mobilized to fight the flames. Pumps and buckets were used to pour water on the burning palace. Anyone who has visited the Museum of London and seen the pathetic size of a late seventeenth-century fire engine (they have one from Windsor Castle there) will realize how pointless this was. The pumps produced no more than a dribble, and people could not get close enough with buckets to make them effective. Remembering the efficacy of gunpowder in fighting the 1691 fire, orders were given to detonate explosives at strategic points to create a firebreak. Twenty enormous explosions rocked the evening air, but to no avail. Burning timber baulks fell on parts that were not yet ablaze, spreading the fire rather than confining it.

Meanwhile the palace servants were evacuating the fabulous works of art, tapestries and paintings from the staterooms. They were all laid out under guard in the palace gardens. Their work was impeded by looters, who climbed over the palace walls hoping to scoop treasures from under the noses of the palace guards. The confusion was increased by the hundreds of private residents of the palace who were intent on saving their goods too. Often the firefighters could not get near the buildings for the press of people attempting to save their personal possessions. Amidst the chaos there were terrible casualties: a grenadier guard was burnt to death, a gardener blown up, and a painter rescuing works of art crushed by a falling iron beam. The Dutch maid who had started the fire was burnt to death too.

The fire raged for fifteen hours and was only extinguished by lunchtime the next day. Yet the firemen should not have gone home so soon, because a gentle breeze the next day reignited the fire in the remains of James's Catholic chapel. The second day's blaze was as bad as the day before, but this time concentrated on the north-west corner, near the Holbein Gate. On William III's express orders, huge efforts were made to save the Banqueting House. Its southern window was bricked up to prevent the flames breaking through into it. After a second day the flames, with little left to burn, died down, leaving Europe's largest palace a pile of rubble.

The Banqueting House was where William and Mary had accepted the offer of the English throne. It was where Charles II had returned in triumph in 1660. It was where Charles I had been executed. And indeed James I had built it as a celebration of Stuart rule. For all these reasons William felt that this great symbol could not be allowed to burn. As for the rest, he was indifferent. He wrote to a Dutch friend, 'the loss is less to me than it would be to another person, for I cannot live there'. Yet the destruction of Whitehall was a blow to national pride, and perhaps as a reaction to this William vowed 'if God would give him leave he would rebuild [Whitehall] much finer than before'. But in the immediate aftermath of the fire there were much more pressing needs. As we have seen, Whitehall housed several important offices of state which required relocating if the work of government was to continue smoothly. Wren was ordered to quickly set up rooms in the old west-side recreation centre for the Treasury and the Council of Trade, and as a Council Chamber. A series of rooms were also set aside for the King, including a privy chamber, drawing room, bedchamber and two closets. The Secretary to the Treasury was provided with an office, and a new meeting room was constructed for the Lords of the Treasury.

We should be in no doubt that William III seriously intended to rebuild Whitehall Palace bigger and better than before. The drawings for a new palace that survive are the result of considerable thought and work and were not completed on a whim. The designs represented, for Wren, the possibility of fulfilling his greatest dream: creating a palace at Whitehall on a European scale. We must remember that designing a new Whitehall was his first royal commission, even before he was in the employ of Charles II, and was also the prime reason for his seminal trip to Paris in 1665. To be given the chance to rebuild Whitehall in 1698 was a dream come true.

Despite Wren's scheme, the completion of Hampton Court and Kensington and magnificent plans for Windsor Castle left little time or money for such a mammoth project, and in any case William died in 1702. His successor, Queen Anne, also entertained the possibility of rebuilding the palace: ''Tis said that her majesty . . . designs to rebuild whitehall, and for that purpose will set aside £100,000 per anum out of her revenue, which will finish the same in 6 years.' In fact, neither Queen Anne nor her successors had anything like £100,000 to spare for palace-building. As a result, whilst the monarchies of Continental Europe built magnificent new palaces for themselves, the kings and queens of England were forced to be content with the palace of St James.

The former site of Whitehall thus lay bare and reproachful from 1698 on. The Banqueting House was converted into a chapel for William III, and he attended a service there on Christmas Day 1698. Close to the Banqueting House stood the Holbein Gate which survived for more than sixty years after the fire, only to be demolished in 1759 to ease the flow of traffic on Whitehall. The rest of the palace site, including Scotland Yard, was gradually leased out to noblemen who slowly converted, demolished and replaced the remaining Tudor and Stuart buildings and constructed fine town houses on the riverside. In 1938 work to construct what is now known as the Ministry of Defence began. Deep foundations for the new building wiped out almost all the remains of the palace on the east side, leaving almost no trace today of the palace that was, on the eve of its destruction, the largest in Europe.

There is an important postscript to this remarkable story. The

The 1670 survey of Whitehall Palace laid over a modern street plan illustrating the vast area covered by the palace in the seventeenth century.

temporary measure to remove government offices from the ruins of Whitehall and relocate them in the recreation centre ended up being a permanent solution. If you are lucky enough to get inside 70 Whitehall, which is the Cabinet Office, you are suddenly transported back into the Tudor palace of Whitehall. For there, today, are still the remains of Henry VIII's tennis courts and bowling alley. In fact in a room in the basement of 10 Downing Street, now used as a library, a section of Tudor wall can be clearly seen. The heart of modern British government beats amongst the remains of Whitehall Palace, and modern parliamentary democracy grew directly out of its ruins. Whitehall Palace may be a lost building, but its ghost haunts the corridors of power to this very day.

Fonthill Abbey

Gothic Dream or Gothic Nightmare?

The words Fonthill Abbey, even today, inspire in many people a shiver of excitement. This enormous country house was possibly the most ambitious and eccentric building project of the whole nineteenth century, which sprang out of the imagination of two of the century's most colourful figures. As the largest building in the Gothic style constructed since the Middle Ages, it helped launch a fashion for Gothic architecture that dominated the Victorian age. Fonthill Abbey and its owner were famous while the Abbey stood but after it had gone both became legendary. So much so that it is now difficult to disentangle the man and the myth, to separate Fonthill fact from Fonthill fiction. Yet few could deny either then or now that Fonthill and its creator were hugely influential. But how did a man who did not even care for Gothic as a style, commission the most famous building of his age and trigger a revival in Gothic architecture that has shaped the appearance of modern Britain? The answer to this question lies in the meeting of two extraordinary men, William Beckford and James Wyatt.

Beckford (see Plate 2) was a legend in his own lifetime, and fascination with his life has remained constant ever since. He has already had nine biographers, and no doubt others will try to capture his bizarre and complex character in the future. His father, Alderman Beckford, sometime Lord Mayor of London, was a famous and extrovert Whig politician; his mother was a complete contrast, a conventional devout Christian, rigid, moral and disapproving. Alderman Beckford had destined William to be a politician, and after his father's early death he was sent to university in Switzerland. On his return something happened that was to change the course of his life. In the summer of 1779, at the age of nineteen, while visiting Lord Courtnay's house, Powderham Castle in Devon, he fell in love with Courtnay's eleven-year-old son, William. Love might be too strong a word: crush, infatuation or obsession might, in fact, serve better. However it is described, though, it is clear that Beckford formed an incredibly strong emotional attachment to young William, whom he soon came to know as Kitty. His obsession with Kitty Courtnay was to dominate his life well beyond his marriage to Lady Margaret Gordon in 1783. In October 1784, long after the relationship with Courtnay had become a passionate physical one, Beckford unwisely, and against the advice of his mother, accepted an invitation from Viscount Courtnay to Powderham Castle. He stayed there, with his wife, for a fortnight. With the passage of time and Beckford's own misleading (and sometimes forged) memoirs and letters we will never know exactly what took place during that extended house party, but it was salacious enough for the newspapers to pick up. Without naming Beckford they suggested that he and Courtnay were lovers – in fact, sodomites – and that Lady Margaret was being degraded by exposure to this moral depravity. What made the situation much worse was that his obsessive love letters to Kitty had fallen into the hands of Courtnay's uncle, Lord Loughborough. Lawyers for the Beckford and Courtnay families became engaged in a tough negotiation over what should happen next. It was probably not in Loughborough's interest to drag William, the Courtnay heir, through the courts to get at Beckford. He may also have feared that Kitty would not have confessed – even if he had done so, as he was as much in love with Beckford as Beckford was with him. So, amazingly, a court case was never brought. If it had been, and if Beckford had been convicted, he would have faced the noose: sodomy still carried the death penalty. Instead Beckford and the pregnant Lady Margaret were ostracized. At first they were isolated at home in Wiltshire, where even their local friends refused to see them. For Beckford, this was intolerable; he had long wanted a peerage (Lord Beckford of Fonthill) and long wanted to go into politics; neither were now a remote possibility. So he, his wife and their newborn baby fled to Switzerland, propelled by the Courtnay lawyers and Mrs Beckford senior's loathing and disapproval.

In Switzerland, after two years, events took a further turn for the worse. In May 1786 Lady Margaret died from complications after childbirth. Inevitably English society and Beckford's own disapproving mother blamed Beckford and what we would now call his bisexual ways. William was devastated and set out on a tour of Europe to expunge his grief. After a brief attempt to return home, vetoed by his mother and by Lord Loughborough's solicitors, Beckford went to Portugal and then France, finally returning to England in 1789. The old Lord Courtnay had died the previous December and the incriminating letters now belonged to Kitty himself, the new Viscount, who of course had no intention of using them. Finally Beckford was safe.

The scandal, his wife's death, education in Switzerland, his enforced exile and the suspicion with which people regarded him ensured that Beckford was always to be an outsider. Yet he had one enormous advantage: he was rich, very, very rich, possibly the richest man in England. Although his wealth fluctuated over his lifetime, the income from his Jamaican sugar estates was constant enough to fuel his astonishingly extravagant lifestyle, to support his lavish foreign trips, to underwrite his passionate collecting and to fuel his megalomaniac desire to build. Beckford, like any rich and educated man of his age, had received an architectural education followed by a Grand Tour of Italy and consolidated by a library of architectural books and prints. But his intensely romantic and obsessive character made it certain that when he turned to architecture it would be with force, passion and originality. He was also to use it to try and polish his tarnished reputation. In 1790 he wrote, 'So I am growing rich and mean to build towers, and sing hymns to the powers of Heaven on their summits.' It was this ambition to build towers that brought him into contact with the most fashionable and successful architect of his day, James Wyatt.

James Wyatt was born into a dynasty of architects and was, as a young man, sent to Italy to learn architectural drawing. While in Rome he caused a sensation by making measured drawings of the

dome of St Peter's Cathedral by lying on his back on a ladder slung
under the dome above a sheer drop of 300 feet. He returned to
England in 1768 with a reputation as a brilliant draftsman but a lazy
and dilatory character. This did not stop him joining the family firm
and learning the practicalities of building from his elder brother,
Samuel. Nor did it stop him carefully observing the most fashionable
architects of their day – the Adam brothers. Soon he had his own
practice and a remarkable reputation for architectural versatility and
originality. Honours came thick and fast and culminated with his
appointment, by King George III, as Surveyor of the Office of
Works – in short, the post of architect royal. Between 1769 and his
death in 1813 he worked on most of the royal palaces, redesigned
and restored five cathedrals and seventeen other churches, directed
works at eight colleges and designed or remodelled over a hundred
country houses. This remarkable and energetic career was blighted
by his dislike of documentation, punctuality, letter-writing, financial control, and all the qualities necessary for pleasing patrons and
administering major building contracts. His laziness was com-
pounded by drunkenness, gluttony and womanizing. He was rid-
iculously over-stretched and his patrons thought him harder to
access than the Prime Minister himself. When he died in a coaching
accident, despite his enormous success he left nothing but debts
and a mortgaged house in the country.

What is remarkable about Wyatt's architecture is its variety.
Unlike so many of our greatest architects, he was not a champion
of a single style and could design equally happily a building in a
Greek style or a Gothic one. As a designer of Gothic Wyatt reigned
supreme. Undoubtedly as the restorer of churches, cathedrals,
Oxford colleges and the old royal palaces he was exposed, more
than any other architect of his age, to Gothic detailing. In this he
became an expert, using his brilliant drafting and observational skills
to produce Gothic designs of sublime beauty. It was this first-hand
knowledge of medieval architecture that set Wyatt's Gothic buildings apart from those that had gone before. The most famous
Gothic house of the previous generation was built by the son of
Robert Walpole, the prime minister. Horace Walpole created, at

A watercolour of Fonthill Splendens by John Buckler from about 1806. The house was built by William Beckford's father in the late 1750s in the latest style, modelled on the house of the prime minister, Sir Robert Walpole, at Houghton in Norfolk.

Strawberry Hill in Twickenham, the first important Gothic mansion in England since the Middle Ages, an essay in a flimsy, but picturesque wedding-cake Gothic. All Wyatt's work was to improve on this in both authenticity of detail and visual substance.

Wyatt and Beckford first got in touch in connection with the house in which Beckford was brought up, a mansion that he had inherited when he was only ten: Fonthill House. This residence, normally known as Fonthill Splendens, was one of the most fashionable houses of its age. It was a vast mansion built in the externally austere Palladian style and furnished inside with the most fashionable decoration of the 1760s. It had a great library, an important picture collection, and carved and gilded furniture. It was also set in a remarkable landscaped park with an artificial lake, grottoes and a beautiful bridge. By the time William reached his twenties this house was regarded by many as heavy, depressing and old fashioned. Its leaden opulence held few delights for young Beckford and so he set out to transform the interiors into the fashionable neoclassical style of the day. William first employed the fashionable young architect John Soane to design him a new picture gallery, before settling on James Wyatt, an architect of greater reputation, as the man to modernize the interiors of Fonthill. Wyatt's skills were supplemented by those of the most fashionable interior decorators from Paris, who designed furniture and ceiling decorations. While this work was under way, and Beckford was in Portugal, Splendens was visited by the Prince Regent, the future George IV, who admired the lavish and fashionable improvements in the latest French style.

Back in England Beckford began to focus on his estate in earnest and just before leaving for his second Portuguese trip in 1793 he began work on a wall 12 feet high and seven miles long to enclose 519 acres around Stops Beacon, the highest point on his estate. It took eighteen months to build, and was intended to form an enclosure centred on a new tower where he could retreat with his books in privacy and solitude. The tower was to be in the Gothic style, then growing increasingly fashionable for isolated buildings in the landscape of great houses. The obvious choice as architect was Wyatt, but inevitably he did not respond in time and Beckford left for Lisbon without seeing a design. Yet the idea did not die and across Europe architect and patron corresponded about Fonthill and about Beckford's house in Lisbon. In one of Wyatt's letters the suggestion was made that Beckford should visit the remarkable and ancient abbey at Batalha. Wyatt knew of this famous Portuguese monastery through drawings of it published from 1792 onwards and perhaps thought that it might provide inspiration not just for a tower but for a 'ruined convent' at Fonthill with enough rooms to use as a retreat.

William Beckford thus left the comforts of Lisbon and set out for the monastery of Batalha. Here in a sleepy valley, surrounded by low hills and peeping out of dense foliage, were the turrets, pinnacles and spires of a medieval monastery. Beckford was entranced by its effect, the combination of landscape and architecture, the feeling of history and picturesque delight. He eagerly explored the church and the abbey buildings and particularly the chapel containing the tomb of the fifteenth-century English princess who had married João I and became Queen Philippa of Portugal. This Gothic mausoleum, decorated with the royal badges of England – fleur-de-lis, leopards and the garter – left a deep impression on Beckford's eye and imagination.

On his return to Fonthill in 1796 work may have already been under way on both a ruined convent and a tower. Certainly by the following year a considerable Gothic structure was under construction with, amongst other things, a great hall, a chapel, a gallery 185 feet long, and a tower 145 feet high. The tower was to be topped by a copy of the mausoleum that Beckford had so admired at Batalha. The first of a number of building disasters struck that winter. An enormous flag, whose pole was strapped to the scaffolding around the growing central tower, was blown so hard by a gale that it brought the whole tower crashing down. Undoubtedly the tower had been built too fast and probably of flimsy materials, and undoubtedly Wyatt was to blame.

The relationship between Beckford and Wyatt was a stormy one, but it was underpinned by mutual respect and a common Romanticism. Respect, however, is not the first word to come to mind when reading Beckford's correspondence. 'Where infamous beast, where are you?' he wrote to Wyatt. 'What putrid inn, what stinking tavern or pox ridden brothel hides your hoary and glutinous limbs?' Beckford gave him the nickname Cloaca, or 'sewer', and railed, 'Who can ever rely on such a person? The atrocious neglect by the great Cloaca cannot lightly be forgiven . . . curse the infamous Bagasse.' Bagasse had originally been the term to describe the waste products from sugar-making, but Beckford knew it also meant whoremonger. Over the centuries since Beckford's death these curse-ridden insults still convey the frustration felt by him in dealing with Wyatt. Wyatt's unreliability was due to his completely dissolute way of life. In March 1804 he left Fonthill, supposedly for London on urgent business. But he pulled his carriage up at a nearby house, unbeknown to Beckford, and stayed there with some friends, slipping into an alcoholic stupor for a day and a half. Beckford later discovered this and flew into a rage. A large part of Wyatt's problem was drink: it may have led to a

stroke; it certainly led to kidney failure. Beckford thought that he
had the 'most watery and pissful tertian Fever. He is of deathly
cadaverousness and stinks as only those beneath ground do.' In
1812, the year before his death, he tried to diet his way back to
health. Beckford noted, 'My Bagasse shows a moderation at the
table worthy of a carthusian monk,' but his complexion was still
bright red, his mind was wandering and he sat silently staring into
thin air.

All Beckford's frustration was, of course, lifted when Wyatt
applied himself to his work. Beckford had an enormous admiration
and respect for Wyatt's skills. In 1812 he raved, 'Every hour, every
moment, he adds some new beauty . . . with a brio, a zeal, an
energy, a faith that would move the largest mountain in the Alps.'
Once, in a frenzy of affection, he wrote, 'My dear, angelic, most
p.p.p.p.perfect Bagasse . . . [is] killing himself with work.' But it
certainly has to be admitted that Wyatt's skills markedly declined
towards the end of his life and Beckford's own summation of his
life is a fine epitaph: 'Alas, my poor Bagasse had already sunk from
the plane of genius to the mire; and for some years now has only
dabbled in the mud.'

Yet in 1796 Wyatt was in his prime and the collapse of the tower
triggered revisions in the design, an expansion of the accommodation, and plans for an even higher and more ambitious tower. By
this stage the idea of a ruined convent had grown so large in
Beckford's mind that he began to contemplate the demolition of
Splendens and the conversion of the 'convent' into an 'abbey' that
would become his principal home. Not only was his father's house
old fashioned, but he disliked its eighteenth-century setting in the
valley near a lake. Instead he wanted his house to be within the
walled estate, where he could create a new Garden of Eden, a lost
domain like the valley of Batalha, with the jewel of his Abbey set
in its midst. It would be a fairyland setting for his life.

Beckford was also to claim that one of the reasons for the
demolition of Splendens and the erection of the Abbey was to
provide work for local craftsmen and labourers. It is true that he
enjoyed mixing with the craftsmen at work on his mansion, and

his sense of social responsibility for his tenants and employees was demonstrated on Twelfth Night 1797. Beckford gave a great Christmas party for the 300 workmen on site and for 400 poor of the locality in front of the condemned Splendens. They feasted at seven long tables (each sitting 100 people) erected in a vast tent. On the menu were an ox and ten sheep roasted whole over an open-air fire while other great bonfires warmed the guests. Spectators, who had come from far and wide, were given bread and beer on the periphery. Beckford, with a select band of gentlemen and ladies, was seated in a Turkish tent in front of the house. The house itself was brought into use to provide dining rooms for his tradesmen, tenants and others. Between the main tent and the Turkish tent was an arena where the workmen and locals wrestled, played football and ran relay races. There were fourteen toasts. James Wyatt proposed the thirteenth, 'May the great work at Fonthill be successfully accomplished!' and the fourteenth was, 'May the ears of John Bull never be insulted by the gipsey jargon of France!'

As the idea of the Abbey grew in his mind Beckford saw the possibilities of using a new house both for the display of his remarkable collections and as a vehicle for contemporary art. Soon he was to be commissioning sculpture from the most famous living sculptors, John Flaxman and Richard Westmacott, and paintings from artists such as Benjamin West and J. M. W. Turner. It was rumoured that he had set aside £60,000 to purchase modern works of art for the house. In 1798 Beckford went to Portugal for a third time, but left behind a building at Fonthill that was inhabitable. Wyatt had completed an octagonal tower that was to be a chapel, built in front of this on a lower level, a banqueting hall, and at right angles to it a single gallery as the new library. At the end of the gallery was a Gothic villa in which Beckford could stay, if he chose.

James Wyatt was commissioned to continue the work while Beckford was abroad: he even rode down to Falmouth to see him off, talking of new improvements all the way. As Beckford sailed Wyatt clutched instructions for a modified, taller tower capable of containing Beckford's tomb (terrified of death, he did not want to be buried underground), a second gallery to balance the first and a new chapel at its end. Wyatt exhibited his plans at the Royal Academy in London in the summer of 1799. When Beckford returned he was not happy with what he saw. The workmen, as usual, had been progressing unsupervised; Wyatt was working on other jobs and wasting his time in bars and brothels. Beckford entered his octagonal tower and looked with horror on the plain, not Gothic, balustrades erected by the workmen. Soon he was on the balcony, back against the wall and feet on the offending balustrade: a heavy shove brought it crashing down. Two hundred feet below furniture was pulverized in a fog of stone dust. Not only does this incident show the tensions between architect and patron and Beckford's passion for detail; it illustrates Wyatt's continuing inability to design and supervise the construction of a tower that would stay up.

The upper parts of the new tower were in fact all in timber and on 17 May 1800 a strong gale brought the tower crashing down for a second time. By then this was national news. Such was the fame of Fonthill, such was the curiosity it aroused, that the collapse was reported in *The Times*. One collapse was a misfortune, but two was carelessness. Beckford was furious with his architect. Wyatt was blamed for poor design, shoddy workmanship and inadequate supervision, and summoned to Fonthill forthwith.

Part of the difficulty had been Wyatt's use of a new type of external render known as 'Roman cement'. During the eighteenth century builders and architects had experimented with various mixtures of lime and volcanic earths in an attempt to discover the recipe that the Romans had used to produce a wall render that looked exactly like stone. In 1796 James Parker of Northfleet patented a recipe for a new type of quick-setting cement that looked exactly like stone. It was waterproof and very strong and could set within as little as half an hour. Wyatt seized upon Parker's new cement as the solution to creating 'stone' walls quickly and cheaply, and all the first phases of Fonthill made extensive use of it. Much of the building was either timber-framed with thin laths of chestnut rendered in Roman cement, or more sturdily (but still ephemerally) built of rendered rubble. The workmen mixed the cement on site and would urinate on the mixture to improve its adhesion to the walls. The top coats were pressed and polished to a fine finish with the flat of a plasterer's trowel. While it was still soft enough, the surface of the render was lined out with a blunt metal tool in order to create faux masonry joints. As it hardened but before it had finally set, coloured sands would be gently pressed into the damp surface in order to give colour variation and texture to the surface. This process was charmingly called 'promiscuous tinting' and achieved a staggeringly realistic surface finish. It was the use of these techniques that enabled Fonthill to rise so very fast, and to collapse for a second time. Although Roman cement looked realistic it had no inherent strength, and the timber substructure could not support its weight.

The second collapse seems to have chastened Wyatt, and he made some significant changes to his design before spurring the workmen on again. So fast did they work that by the end of the year the house was nearly ready to use. Here was the moment that Beckford had waited for, a chance to use his remarkable mansion to regain some social credibility. His plan was to entertain the most famous man in England, a man touched, like himself, with a sex scandal and who, like himself, was an outsider. This was the victor of the Battle of the Nile, the greatest admiral of his age – Lord Nelson himself. Beckford planned to host a house party for the Admiral and to make its culmination a dinner at the Abbey. This dinner was intended to establish the Abbey as a social centre and Beckford as a society host.

There were only a small number of guests: Nelson and his notorious mistress Lady Hamilton, wife of the British Consul in Naples; her husband Sir William Hamilton; the famous American painter Benjamin West; James Wyatt, the creator of the Abbey; and a handful of Beckford's closest companions. One of the reasons that Nelson had accepted the invitation to stay over Christmas was that the party would be small, so he would not be pestered by a large house party of adoring fans. They were accommodated at Fonthill Splendens, since the Abbey was far from ready to accommodate

A print from the *Gentleman's Magazine* showing Lord Nelson's carriage wending its way to Fonthill Abbey from Fonthill Splendens for the famous Christmas dinner of 1800.

even a modest house party such as this, but as dusk fell on 23 December they were transported by carriage up the hill to the new Abbey. Normally the trip would have taken ten minutes but an elaborate route had been devised, stretching the trip to three-quarters of an hour. The serpentine route was lined with horsemen bearing flaming torches, and lanterns strung in the trees. Hidden in the woods were drummers and musicians who heightened the atmosphere by playing their instruments as the carriage

procession passed. Occasionally a cannon was fired to heighten the
sense of anticipation (and perhaps make Nelson feel at home).
When they arrived at the Abbey it was lit by an array of special
lanterns and torches to exaggerate its mystery and scale. The smoke
they gave off wafted up around the tower, so it looked as if it
disappeared into the clouds. Dinner was held in the great hall on
the west side at a 53-foot-long table beneath a minstrels' gallery
from where the guests were serenaded. Dinner itself was medieval,
according to a contemporary report, 'unmingled with any of the
refinements of the modern culinary art'. In fact they ate from
medieval-style trenchers, that is to say slabs of rock-hard stale bread,
and drank from horn beakers. The food was a series of meat dishes
without the fashionable creamy sauces of the day. After dinner they
retired upstairs. On the stairs there were hooded 'monks' holding
large wax tapers. In the Yellow Drawing Room there were sweetmeats, spices and wine. There Emma Hamiltion performed her
'attitudes', a series of mime tableaux of classical figures posturing.
Not what we would today regard as after-dinner entertainment,
but at the time the height of sophistication and elegance. The
dinner was not a success: Emma was eight months pregnant and
famed for her love of good food and wine. Dinner, by her standards,
was revolting, and the great hall in midwinter was freezing. Nelson
cannot have thought much more of it – he certainly did not accept
another invitation to stay (although he entertained Beckford at his
London house for dinner). But this is to miss the point historically.
It was a remarkable occasion in the history of the Gothic revival in
England – probably the first neo-Gothic feast, and one widely
reported in the papers. The *Gentleman's Magazine* gave several pages
to describing the event and even produced an illustration of it. As
usual with William Beckford, all was illusion and publicity: the
fame of the event was as important as the happening itself.

   Perhaps it was the inconveniences of the Nelson visit, or maybe
even the pleasures of it, that convinced Beckford to turn the Abbey
into a full-blown residence. The side wings at Splendens were
demolished to provide building stone and two great auctions sold
off furniture and paintings that were not required for the new

project. But his ambitions were slowed by financial difficulties and the great project was put on hold for a period of three years. When work started again in 1805 more problems were found with the tower. The Roman cement that Wyatt had used to propel the tower to 300 feet was falling off the timber framework and threatened another collapse. Beckford finally tired of Wyatt's cheap methods and employed a gang of stonemasons from London to rebuild the upper parts of the tower in stone, causing more delay and even greater expense. Soon Beckford decided to demolish the remaining parts of Splendens and concentrate his entire efforts on the Abbey; this allowed him to finally move in during the summer of 1807.

Despite the fact that Beckford was now living at the Abbey, work continued. Ignoring the advice of his lawyer, who could see the strain continual construction was causing Beckford's bank account, work began on the east wing. In August 1812 he wrote to a friend, 'Some people drink to forget their unhappiness. I do not drink. I build. And it ruins me. It would be cheaper to find another distraction.' Nevertheless Beckford kept on building; not even the death of James Wyatt in September 1813 could stop him now. In fact his architect's death triggered another phase. Beckford accelerated the replacement of much of Wyatt's timberwork and Roman cement with well-cut stone. The tiny fragment that survives today shows that much of the Abbey was reclad in high-quality finely-jointed masonry fixed together with metal cramps.

The completed house was in the shape of a cross with the octagonal tower at the crossing point, not unlike a medieval cathedral. From north to south the cross measured 312 feet, about the length of Westminster Abbey. From west to east it was 270 feet. It was entered from a vast entrance hall on the west that was aligned on a great avenue of trees nearly a mile long in the park. The entrance door itself was 30 feet tall and tended by a dwarf. This was Pierre de Grailly, whom Beckford had met in Madrid and employed for life. The contrast between Pierre and the door emphasized the principal feature of the Abbey, which was the exaggerated scale of its elements, all designed to create a sense of

The Lancaster Tower, the only surviving part of the Abbey today.

awe and wonder, if not a little terror too. The entrance hall was
vaulted over by a plaster 'hammer-beam' roof modelled on the oak
roof in the great hall of Hampton Court Palace. This was originally
meant to be the Abbey's dining room (it was where Nelson dined)
but the room was absurdly large and cold for sitting still in and was
later converted into an entrance hall. At the far end of the hall a
flight of stairs led up to the Octagon Hall at the centre of the Abbey.
The Octagon was at first called the 'Cardinal's Parlour' and was

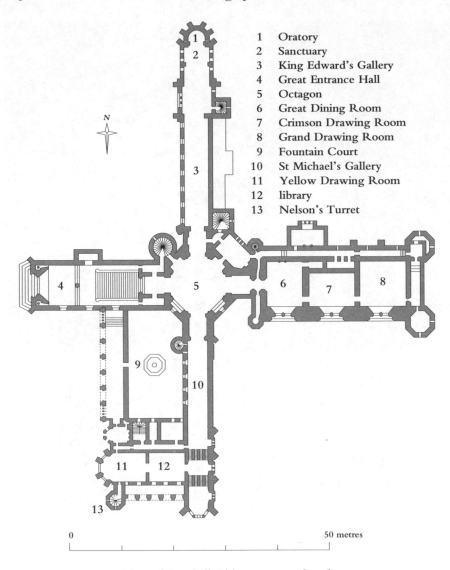

1   Oratory
2   Sanctuary
3   King Edward's Gallery
4   Great Entrance Hall
5   Octagon
6   Great Dining Room
7   Crimson Drawing Room
8   Grand Drawing Room
9   Fountain Court
10 St Michael's Gallery
11 Yellow Drawing Room
12 library
13 Nelson's Turret

0   50 metres

Plan of Fonthill Abbey as completed.

hung with tapestries with curtains of purple damask over the 50-foot-tall windows; ebony and ivory furniture was set round the room and silver sconces provided a flickering light from the walls. Over 250 feet above the floor was Wyatt's magnificent timber ceiling with painted heraldic shields. Twenty feet above that, crowning the top, were the pinnacles of the tower.

John Rutter's view of Fonthill from the south in 1823. The Great Entrance Hall is on the far left, with the Yellow Drawing Room and the library in front.

Two galleries, each over 100 feet long, one named after King Edward III and the other after St Michael, lay to the north and south of the Octagon. St Michael's Gallery was one of the most magnificent interiors in the house, vaulted with fan vaults (see Plate 4). These vaults were something of a trademark of the early Gothic revival. They were inspired by the vaulting at Henry VII's Chapel at Westminster and the chapel at King's College, Cambridge, which were, rightly, considered masterpieces of Gothic stonemasonry. Of course no one in Regency England had ever made a stone vault and so Wyatt's were purely stage dressing in timber and plaster, painted to look like stone. An oriel window at the end of the gallery gave a spectacular view over the grounds and down towards a lake. Bookcases were set into the walls and above these were curtain rails from which blue and red curtains were

John Rutter's view of the Great Entrance Hall of Fonthill Abbey in 1823. Originally the dining room, a stair led up from it to the Octagon, the hub of the Abbey.

hung. On the other side of the central Octagon was King Edward's Gallery, decorated with a dark oak ceiling in low relief. The walls were hung with red damask and a frieze contained the badges of seventy-eight knights of the garter, from whom Beckford was supposedly descended. Over the fireplace was a portrait of Edward III himself. At the end of the gallery was the Vaulted Corridor, a dark space with a beautiful coved ceiling covered in latticework. Beyond this was the Sanctuary, entered through doors that magically opened when Beckford shouted 'Open!' (and stamped on a concealed footpad). Finally at the far end was the holy of holies, the Oratory, a gilded shrine dedicated to St Anthony of Padua, filled with priceless jewelled reliquaries set against the richest textiles and gloomily illuminated through the most lustrous stained glass.

Stained glass windows were an important part of the Abbey's design, filtering the sunlight into a multicoloured blaze on the carpets and furniture and creating the sombre gloom that was considered one of the primary constituents of the Gothic style. Most of the new glass was made by Francis and William Eginton, who supplied thirty-two windows at a cost of £12,000. There was antique glass too, mainly Renaissance Flemish pieces, set into the windows. In Bristol, close to the town hall, is the ravishing little chapel of St Mark, the Lord Mayor's Chapel. In here is some of Beckford's antique glass but, even more importantly, one of the windows originally designed for the Abbey (and installed in the Beckett Room) by Benjamin West in 1799.

Another key part of the decoration of the Abbey was heraldry, also and rightly seen as a key component of medieval architecture. Beckford employed the Garter King of Arms, the chief herald, to research the heraldry necessary to decorate the walls, ceilings, carpets, even books, with his arms. For modern-day collectors this means that a Beckford library book is easy to spot, and very valuable.

The whole Abbey, when completed, was essentially an art gallery and library containing one of the greatest collections ever amassed by a private individual in England. A network of dealers, together with his circle of painters and sculptors, scouted for the finest works of art across Europe. Wyatt himself was instrumental in helping

John Rutter's 1823 cross section of the completed Abbey. This drawing not only shows the interiors, but provides crucial clues as to why the tower collapsed. The Oratory and Sanctuary are on the first floor on the far left, with King Edward's Gallery linking them to the central Octagon. St Michael's Gallery leads from this to the Yellow Drawing Room on the far right.

Drawn by C.F. Porden, Arch.

acquire many of the finest pieces. Beckford's taste was predominantly French. To us this might seem inexplicable, given the political climate of the age. France had undergone an amazingly brutal and bloody revolution in 1789. This had led directly to the assumption of power by the Emperor Napoleon Bonaparte who

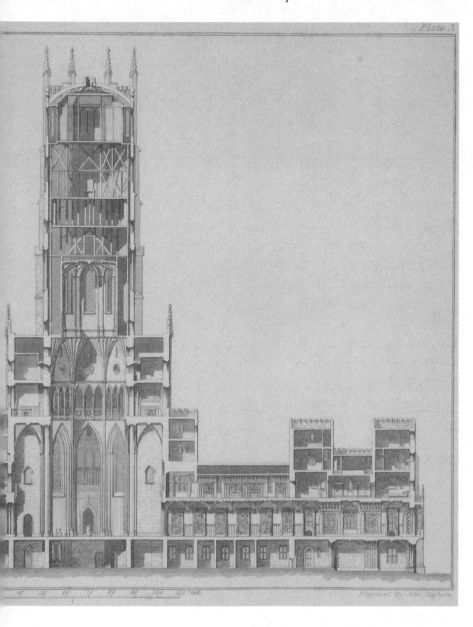

had terrorized Europe and assembled a force of 80,000 troops to invade England. The English establishment not only feared invasion by France but also a bloody popular revolution on English soil. Yet Beckford was not alone in regarding French fashions as the finest and most desirable – the Prince Regent himself, soon to be King

George IV, furnished his houses with the finest in French furniture and textiles too. Items Beckford bought that were not French themselves may, in many cases, have come from great collections assembled by the cognoscenti of France. The provenance of his works of art gave them added interest, value and romantic appeal. The collection included ivories, lacquerwork, porcelain, silver and gold, precious stones, glassware, intaglios, manuscripts, rare books, coins, carpets, paintings and furniture. Items were mainly Renaissance or medieval and their rarity and beauty were more important than their authenticity: ultimately Beckford was interested in the effect of the whole ensemble set against the backdrop of the Abbey.

Other than wrestling with Wyatt and instructing his craftsmen and artists, arranging and rearranging this collection was Beckford's principal recreation. He believed 'Everything depends on the way objects are placed, and where. Horrors in one place discount beauties in another.' Most of the collection was displayed in or on cabinets that were placed all over the house. There was no attempt to keep types of object together: in fact everything was mixed up for the best effect. When visitors came, which was rare, they would most likely be artists, and their time would be spent admiring works of art and Beckford's arrangement of them. Understanding the importance of Beckford's collection is the key to understanding the Abbey: architecture and objects were a single work of art; the building had no point without the collection – it was, in many senses, simply a grand showcase for it. But there is another aspect to Beckford's genius, for just as the building and its collection were the product of a single vision, so was the landscape in which the Abbey sat. The Abbey had started off as a garden folly, and throughout its expansion into a monstrous country house it remained inextricably linked to its landscape both in concept and execution.

The driving force behind the Fonthill landscape was a rejection of the landscape of Splendens with its lawns rolling down to a manicured lake punctured by artistically grouped clumps of trees. Beckford wanted to create a wilder and more romantic landscape, avoiding the rigid avenues and artificial tricks of Capability Brown.

Another strong influence was that of Switzerland, where he had spent so much time in his youth. Alpine trees, such as firs and pines, and alpine flowering shrubs – even log cabins – formed part of his conception. An easy way to understand what he was trying to achieve is to walk down the great western drive, nearly a mile long, that led to the Abbey's front door. Unlike most houses of the previous generation, whose avenues would have been made up of trees of one species rigidly planted in a regular rhythm, the Fonthill avenue was a slash in the woods, a green sward between clumps of trees and shrubs that gradually widened as it neared the Abbey.

Through the landscape was cut a long winding path, Nine Miles Walk, a sinuous circuit of grassy paths that wove their way to every vantage point within the walled estate. It was a brilliantly planned tour of the estate with variety in light and shade, hills and valleys, smooth lawns and rough wildernesses. The trees either side were mainly native – a million of them, oak, birch, larch underplanted with hazel, holly and thorns. Where the land fell away to the south Beckford created a lake. Bitham Lake was originally a fishpond but was excavated further and dammed by Beckford. Its banks were lovingly contoured to create a picturesque effect, perhaps like a Swiss lake. Wildfowl were encouraged to swoop down from the trees and land on the water. Gaps were cut in the trees so that it could be seen from the Abbey and other key vantage points. On the eastern side of the lake was the American garden, planted with rhododendrons, magnolias and azaleas – at the time rare imports from America.

There was also a Chinese garden devoted to oriental flowers; a flower garden with a range of hothouses 450 feet long filled with rare and exotic fruits and flowers; a kitchen garden; and a herb garden devoted to growing monastic herbs. Collecting plants and trees was as much of an obsession as collecting works of art or building the Abbey itself, and Beckford's knowledge and taste in horticulture were as sure as in architecture or connoisseurship.

By 1820 Beckford was caught in a terrible financial pincer. On the one hand the costs of Fonthill had spiralled, and rebuilding Wyatt's ill-constructed tower alone had cost £30,000. On the

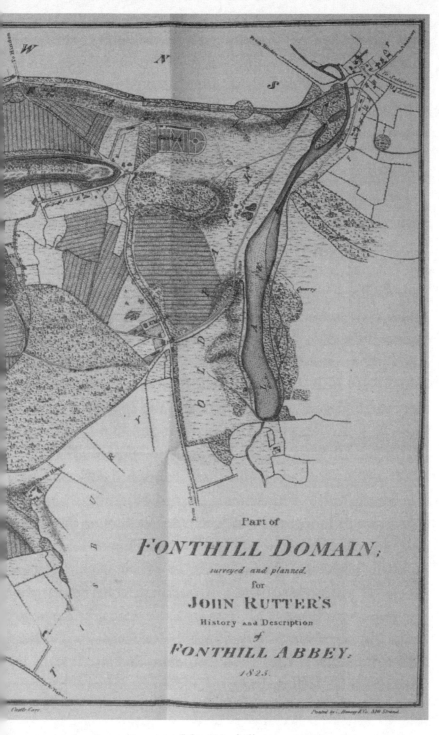

John Rutter's map of the Fonthill estate in 1823.

other, his revenue from Jamaican sugar had slumped. Disputes over the ownership of his estates, the falling price of sugar, and uncertainty over the use of slaves had reduced his income to a trickle of its former volume. For the first time he was forced to make real economies. English land was sold, the size of his establishment was reduced and his spending spree curbed. In the midst of all this Beckford began to tire of the Abbey. Not only was it absorbing all his finances, not only was Wyatt's appalling structural legacy making the building look unviable in the long term, but it was horrible to live in. The enormous size of the rooms made it cold both in winter and summer; gales blew through the corridors and damp gripped Beckford's bones. Sixty fires had to be kept continually burning winter and summer to keep the house dry, let alone warm. His food must have been served cold, day after day: the oak parlour, where he normally dined, was miles from the kitchens. The eighteen bedrooms were reached by narrow spiral stairs of enormous height, making houseguests wary of accepting an invitation – even if the reclusive Beckford were to offer one. In fact thirteen of the bedrooms were unventilated and virtually unusable. There were no bells in the house to summon servants and so one of them had to wait outside each door, enormously increasing the already vast running costs. Beckford said he hated the 'blasts of wind, blasts of cold, blasts of rheum and financial blasts in this uninhabitable place'. In spring 1822, to everyone's amazement, he announced that the Abbey and its contents were up for sale. James Christie the auctioneer issued a catalogue listing the thousands of items of furniture, pictures and works of art. The sale was to be in September and viewing was to start on 1 July.

Society was catapulted into a frenzy. Suddenly the man with a reputation for being England's richest, the man who had built the most famous house of his day, the man who had assembled a world-famous collection, was throwing it open to the public. So few had seen behind the twelve-foot walls of the Fonthill boundary that this was the hottest ticket in town. Fonthill Fever struck. Thousands of people made their way to Wiltshire in carriages and by horse hoping for a glimpse of the house, the collections, and hopefully the man himself. Each day up to seventy carriages arrived at the front door disgorging the rich, the famous or simply the curious. Amongst them were the King's brother-in-law, the Duke of Gloucester, and the Duke of Wellington, who claimed that he had seen nothing in all Europe to compare with the house. Local accommodation was at a premium: inns, taverns and even private houses for miles around were booked for weeks in advance. By the end of the viewing 72,000 people had toured the Abbey.

This frenzy prompted the publication of three guidebooks to the house, its grounds and the collections. The rival publications vied to be the definitive account of the Abbey's glories. The most successful was by John Rutter, who wrote two books on Fonthill that rapidly went through six editions. His rival was the antiquarian John Britton who wrote *Graphical and Literary Illustrations of Fonthill Abbey*.

The visitors, the press coverage, the guidebooks, the fame and acclaim went to Beckford's head. He wrote to his son-in-law, 'The rage is at its height. They dream of the Abbey, they talk only of it. I doubt whether since the beginning of printing they have ever uttered such extravagances.' What is interesting about all this was the part that Beckford himself played. He was the Svengali behind much of the hype. He helped both Rutter and Britton with their rival guides, he enlisted the help of his literary friends to place articles in the *Literary Gazette*, the *Gentleman's Magazine* and elsewhere. He fully understood that Fonthill Fever would buoy the price he would get for the Abbey. In the autumn in 1822 he wrote, 'I think the Public will gladly swallow it up, for they are beginning to busy themselves with the Abbey, and they even seem disposed to pane-gyrize everything about it.' In fact Beckford was angling to avoid an auction sale at all. What he really wanted was to sell the whole estate, building contents and all, to a single buyer. To allow this to happen the viewings were extended and the sale delayed twice.

James Christie arrived at the Abbey on Monday 7 October, the day before the sale was to be held. Everything was in place and buyers were poised to descend on the Abbey the next morning. It was then that Beckford dropped a bombshell. He told Christie that he had cancelled the sale, and through the good offices of a rival auctioneer, Mr Phillips, had sold the house, contents and all, to one John Farquhar. The anticlimax was palpable, Christie was furious and embarrassed, many of the public felt cheated and duped, but Farquhar and Beckford were happy.

James Farquhar was a Scottish gunpowder magnate with major financial interests in brewing (he owned most of the Whitbread brewery). He had been whipped into a frenzy by Fonthill Fever and saw his purchase of the notorious estate as an instant passport to acceptance by English society: Fonthill Abbey was once again to be used by an outsider as a ticket to social success. They drew up a complicated sale contract that reserved to Beckford a small number of choice items, most of his family heirlooms and half of the 20,000 books. The contract took some months to ratify but by early 1823 £300,000 was safely in Beckford's bank account. His debts were paid and with the considerable balance he purchased a house in Bath and a building plot on top of neighbouring Lansdown Hill where he built a tower as a retreat for himself.

Beckford's Fonthill collection did not stay intact for long. Later that year Farquhar asked Mr Phillips to conduct an auction of most of the contents. Fonthill Fever was back and people once again flocked to see the remarkable house and its collections. The sale of books and prints took twenty days, and was surrounded by controversy as Phillips was accused of adding new books to the collection to boost his profits. The following days were reserved for furniture and works of art and on the last day the contents of the wine cellar were sold.

Farquhar was now installed as the new Abbot of Fonthill and he proceeded to entertain his guests there in a series of house parties. These must have been frightening occasions for it was obvious to most people that the tower was still very unstable despite all that Beckford had done to shore it up. On one occasion, during a storm, the creaks and cracking coming from the upper parts of the tower were so bad that the guests fled from their rooms round the tower's base and spent the rest of the night huddled together on the ground floor. On 21 December 1825 the inevitable happened. Farquhar

John Buckler's view of Fonthill Abbey in ruins in 1829. It can be seen that despite the catastrophic fall of the tower much of the Abbey remained standing.

was wheeled in his bath chair to the front of the building to get a close look at some cracks that had appeared that day in the tower. Although it was leaning slightly to the south-west he returned to his rooms unconcerned at the risk of a collapse. It was the most foolhardy thing he had ever done, for a few minutes later, with grace and state, the great tower sank downwards and then burst out to the south-west where these were no other buildings to brace it. Amazingly neither Farquhar nor his servants heard the fall, although one was blown 30 feet along a corridor by the blast of air. A huge cloud of dust hung over the site and the Abbey was largely reduced to a ruin.

Farquhar was alleged to remark that the destruction of a third of the Abbey made it more manageable to live in, and Beckford is said to have observed that the tower that had never bowed to him, had to his successor. But this was the end of the Abbey's story. It remained in ruins after Farquhar's death and until Beckford's own death in 1844. Most of the materials were then carted away and the sole surviving fragment, the Lancaster Tower, was turned into a garden folly. What had originally sprung out of the romantic imagination of a dreamer was now truly a romantic ruin. A vast Gothic cadaver reeking of Beckford's great collections, the Nelson dinner and Wyatt's majestic interiors lay forlorn, but certainly not forgotten. The Abbey, as we shall see, has been a source of inspiration and curiosity ever since.

When we decided to include Fonthill in the television series *Lost Buildings of Britain*, we decided to clear up the mystery of why the great tower finally fell – a topic that has generated a huge amount of print and speculation. The reason normally given for its collapse was that Wyatt's workmen did not dig deep enough foundations. So we decided to test this theory with one of my colleagues, Keith Weston, a historic buildings engineer from English Heritage. We could not dig the site up, but we gained permission to use a ground-penetrating radar that could give us a cross section of the foundations of the Abbey, if they still existed. They did, and the scan showed that in fact they were over 2 metres deep and very wide and solidly packed (see Plate 5). Clearly Wyatt's men had built a good foundation for the Abbey from the start. Keith Weston then analysed Rutter's excellent cross section of the Abbey. What this showed was that the lower walls of the tower were far too thin for the weight of masonry that they had to support. It was these that gave way beneath pressure from above, explaining why at first the tower sank vertically before falling sideways. That this happened at all was thus probably not entirely Wyatt's fault. The tower that he left before his death was made of relatively light materials. Admittedly they were ephemeral and needed replacing if the Abbey was to survive. But his tower was founded solidly and the weight:height ratio was probably stable. Beckford's replacement of the original materials with stone was a mistake. As the upper levels were rebuilt in more solid materials after Wyatt's death, the lower walls of the tower were overloaded and prone to collapse. This is what they eventually did, under the weight of a tower they were never designed to take. In my view Wyatt was largely exonerated, and

Beckford had only himself to blame. But Beckford showed no public regret, no shame and certainly no sense of responsibility for the collapse. This was a chapter of his life that was now closed.

As it closed another opened, one that he had not intended to write, let alone inspire: the Gothic revival. The impact that Fonthill had on Wyatt's career is undeniable. Wyatt became the leading architect in the Gothic style and an amazing number of important commissions flowed in his direction. In fact thanks to his work for King George III at Windsor Castle and at Kew (now lost), the King himself became England's greatest patron of the Gothic, setting a seal of approval on the style. Wyatt's brilliant command of Gothic detailing can be seen at his only significant surviving building in the Gothic style, Ashridge House in Hertfordshire. The house is often open to the public and here we can get closest today to Fonthill. Yet it was not only through Wyatt that Fonthill's power was exercised. Architects and artists all admired it for its emotional effects: in the summer, its sublime beauty set in the landscape, and in winter its demonic power against stormy skies. It became an inspiration to a generation of builders and designers. Its influence can ultimately be traced to Britain's largest and most important Gothic revival building, the Palace of Westminster, better known as the Houses of Parliament.

In 1799 Wyatt, over the head of the classical architect Sir John Soane, won the commission to remodel the House of Lords and to harmonize the ramshackle old buildings that then made up the Palace of Westminster. He won the job largely through the championship of his royal patron, George III. His buildings did not last long: the whole palace was engulfed in a great fire in 1834. By that date there was little debate as to which style should be used for their reconstruction and the parliamentary committee in charge of the rebuilding ordered that the design should be Gothic or Elizabethan. These medieval styles were by then regarded as the national style of architecture, the only styles that could represent the ancient liberties of the English people. This was the first public building of the Gothic revival and the chosen architect, Charles Barry, turned for inspiration to the largest and most influential building yet built in the Gothic style – Fonthill Abbey. The key feature of Fonthill, the long narrow galleries intersected by an octagonal lobby, is at the core of the design for the Houses of Parliament.

The remarkable point about Fonthill is that for a new house it had such an impact, to the degree that it could influence the building of a new seat of government. But it is questionable whether without the character of Beckford himself anyone would have been very interested in Fonthill. It was his scandal-struck youth, rumours of his unorthodoxy and his reclusive tendency that catapulted Fonthill into the public gaze. Yet the most extraordinary thing is that he is remembered for Fonthill at all: in reality it occupied only fifteen years of his 84-year-long life. A life that was, in fact, devoted to Palladian and neoclassical architecture; his Bath tower, the Lansdown Tower, was built in the Greek style. Gothic was a style he never had any real affection for. On visiting Longleat House, where Wyatt's nephew, Jeffrey Wyatt, was working he wrote, 'Throughout this building one recognises the hall mark of Bagasse – his poor lazy methods, his eternal vulgar architraves and false arches etc – a plague of Wyattiana. That infamous style will corrupt all England and like mice and bugs will riddle beds, tables, roofs, walls etc etc.' So if it was not a passion for Gothic that inspired Beckford's Fonthill, what was it? The roots of Fonthill Abbey can be found at Beckford's twenty-first birthday party in 1781 at Splendens. For the occasion William was determined to transform the old place into a magical, romantic realm. He employed the famous stage designer and technician Philippe Jacques de Loutherbourg to install his coloured canvases, gauzes and painted lenses to fill the gaunt halls of Splendens with waterfalls and volcanoes, and rake them with sunrises and sunsets. Incense burners filled the air with exotic smells and trails of smoke, while hidden castrati sang arias. Every recess was filled with tables groaning with fruit and flowers surrounded by rich drapes and curtains. Beckford had created an intense assault on the senses and the imagination: sight, hearing, smell, taste and touch were all under his control, and each sense had to be overwhelmed. This is what the Abbey set out to

Lansdown Tower, or Beckford's Tower, near Bath. This was Beckford's retirement project, constructed in the newly fashionable Greek style.

do, but on a much larger scale. It was an illusion, a stage set. It was not architecture, it was a vast painted canvas against which he could show off his collections. There, thanks to Bagasse, was a total ravishing of the senses: rich colours, light filtered by the stained glass, the distant strains of the organ and the whiff of oriental scents. The transportation of the soul and mind to another era and another place. That transport helped shape the face of Queen Victoria's

Britain, and in due course of her Empire across the world. What started on a hill top in Wiltshire went on to shape the look of a quarter of the globe.

Theatre Royal, Drury Lane

The Crucible of Modern Theatre

A theatre has been in continuous use in Drury Lane for almost three and a half centuries, longer than any other site in Britain, and longer than most in the world. Four buildings on the site of the present theatre have housed some of the most famous theatrical performances ever given, by some of the world's greatest actors and actresses. Of the four theatres one stands out as being perhaps the most important theatre ever built in Britain. Originally designed by Sir Christopher Wren, and given the epithet 'Royal' by Charles II, it remained the home of English theatre for 117 years. For the last twenty-nine years of that time it was managed by the father of modern theatre, David Garrick. Under his rule it became a dynamo of innovation, spinning new ideas across Europe and the world. As a result the Theatre Royal, Drury Lane can genuinely claim to be the birthplace of theatre as we know it today. This great building was demolished in 1791, before the invention of photography, and its appearance and arrangement have long been matters of debate amongst historians and actors. Yet enough information survives to bring this lost building back to life and tell the extraordinary tale of its success.

Throughout the Middle Ages plays, or what we might call theatre, had been tremendously popular with all sectors of society. Like so many aspects of medieval life, theatre was itinerant: groups of players moved from place to place performing in market squares, inn yards, or the houses and castles of the rich. In the Elizabethan period things began to change. London had grown into a vast and comparatively rich city with a population hungry for entertainment and hedonism. The staging of plays in the yards of inns became almost a permanent feature of life. As they did, the managers of

whito Hall stayres

white-hall   Scotland Yard   Suffolk-house   Yorke-house   Durham h   Salsbury h   New Exchange

Somerset h   Arundel

LEX

AD LONDINVM EPITOMEN & OCELLVM.

Nympha Britannorum Regali Sede decora
Totius & Regni Nobilitatis apes.
Quicquid habet sparsum pelago circumfusus
Tu reluces Patriæ Cynthia grata sinus.
Te tuus irradiat sol & tot Sidera Gentis
Cæsar: & ad tubas fert Portans Lucem.
Iustitiæ summum ius patet in te cuique Tribu
Iurisdicumque amplæ nota Theatra, Domus.

Ordo Magistratum subibit ceu cardine picto
Dum capiti præstant singula membra sua docens
Emporium cunctas profert Mercator adultus
Mercei luxusque refert pontus & aura rates
Viribus almæ suos sociat Concordia Cives
Educat & fortes Pallas ad arma Viros
Sic vigeas felix Magno sub Rege Britannus
Floreat ut tantis insula tota bonis.

Serenißimæ MARIÆ invictißimæ magnæ Britanniæ,
Galliæ, Hiberniæ Regis, fidei defensoris filiæ natu maxi:
imæ, felicißimis auspicijs Potentißimo Guilielmo Princi:
pi Auriaco, Comiti Naßavio coniunctæ hunc amœnißi:
mum celeberrimi Londinensis emporij ac sedes regalis
aspectum.

           D. C. Q.   Cornelius Danckers

Wenceslaus Hollar delineauit, et fecit Londini et Antuerpiæ 1647

1 Parlament house
2 Westminster Hal
3 Westminster Abby
4 the Clok house

Engraving by Wenceslaus Hollar showing Elizabethan Bankside
(Southwark), with two major circular theatres in the middle ground.

theatre companies realized that they could significantly increase their profits if they cut out the innkeepers and build their own venues. In the late 1570s and 1580s came the first purpose-built theatres in England. They were circular or octagonal arenas, with tiered covered seating on four or five levels. Their raised stages projected out into the audience, surrounding the actors on three sides with the standing audience or 'groundlings' in the open-air pit. Actors made their entrance from two stage doors located in full view at the back of the stage. There was little opportunity for the use of scenery or sets and all performances had to be carried out in daylight, in the early afternoon; and in the summer. In the early seventeenth century, under the patronage of James I and his court-iers, many companies ran a winter season too, acting in halls or even the royal palaces. It is easy for us today to visualize these theatres, since in 1997 the Globe, possibly the most famous of them all, was rebuilt on the bank of the Thames. For the great halls used for winter theatres we can still go to Middle Temple Hall just off the Strand and see the very room in which performances were held.

It was in theatres such as these that Shakespeare, Christopher Marlowe and Ben Jonson worked. Their audiences comprised most elements of society: apprentices, shopkeepers, craftsmen, lawyers, merchants and civil servants, up to the nobility. The cost of admis-sion to the pit was a penny, a fifth of a labourer's daily wage, while a stool on the stage was sixpence and a box or private room was a shilling. Audiences could be enormous: it is thought that more than 2,000 spectators could have attended performances at the Globe. Indoor playhouses had a similar layout but were rectangular in shape with rows of benches in the stalls. Their seating capacity of around 400 meant that prices were about five times more expensive, creating a more genteel atmosphere.

The great popularity of the theatre under Elizabeth and James I, which had seen seven playhouses established in London, was increasingly undermined by the religious and moral sensibilities of middle-class lawyers, merchants, academics and churchmen, who began to associate the stage with sin, social unrest and moral laxness. They were, of course, right. The theatres were located near brothels, and prostitutes cruised the audiences for clients. Young men went to plays to be seen and to rub shoulders, and more intimate parts, with girls. Drinking, rowdiness and the occasional brawl were all part of an evening out at the theatre. William Prynne, writing in the mid 1630s, thought 'Popular stage plays' were 'the very pomp of the Devil . . . sinful, heathenish, lewd, ungodly spectacles, and most pernicious corruption; condemned in all ages as intolerable mischiefs to churches, to the manners, minds and souls of men.'

These attitudes became official policy as Parliament set itself up as an alternative to Charles I's monarchy. As the Civil War began in 1642, Parliament banned theatre – supposedly until the troubles were over. The Globe Theatre was pulled down in 1644, the Fortune, Phoenix and Salisbury Court theatres in 1649, and Black-friars Theatre in 1655. However Londoners were not to be deprived of their pleasures so easily. The suppression led to more clandestine forms of entertainment: performances in private houses, schools and inns. Drama itself adapted to the times, and Londoners came to enjoy theatre-on-the-run in the form of farces or drolls. These were pared-down versions of popular plays or individual scenes, perfect for quick getaways.

In May 1660 King Charles II returned in triumph from exile to re-establish the monarchy on the crumbled ruins of Oliver Cromwell's austere republic. With him was the future manager of the Theatre Royal, Drury Lane: Thomas Killigrew, courtier, playwright and wit. He told Pepys that his interest in the theatre started when he used to see plays at the Red Bull, a City inn, for free. His wheeze was to be part of the act: 'When the man cried to the boys "who will go and be a devil, and he shall see the play for nothing?" then would he go in, and be a devil upon the stage, and so get to see plays.'

Killigrew was born in 1612, and at the age of twenty-one he joined the court as a page to Charles I. His first and most popular play was a bawdy comedy, *The Parson's Wedding*, but he also wrote and had performed a number of tragedies before the outbreak of the Civil War. At the same time he earned himself a reputation as a reckless spendthrift and womanizer. An engraving, published by Hollar, portrayed him in despair with a monkey perched on his shoulder and dressed in a gown decorated with the recognizable portraits of twenty-four women. Other portraits depicted him in more serious guises surrounded by theatrical scripts. He was imprisoned soon after the start of the Civil War but was released in 1643 and some time afterwards fled to the Continent where he won a second wife with a dowry of £10,000, and hovered around the exiled Charles II, entertaining him with his wit and doubtful taste. It was presumably during this time that he secured a promise to be granted a licence to run a theatre if Charles were ever to reclaim the Crown.

On 25 May 1660 the *Royal Charles* sailed into Dover to be greeted by the great Cromwellian General, Monck and a crowd of joyous subjects. Pepys recorded the mood: 'Infinite the crowd of people and the gallantry of the horsemen, citizens, and noblemen of all sorts . . . The shouting and joy expressed by all is past imagination.' Killigrew had been entertaining the King on deck. Pepys records his jokes but either 350 years or something in the telling makes it almost impossible to find them funny today.

Thanks to the increasingly regal Oliver Cromwell having allowed the performance of a limited number of plays from the mid 1650s, London in 1660 had at least three playhouses. At Drury Lane there was the Cockpit, with a troupe of actors under the management of John Rhodes, a former bookseller. In Clerkenwell, the Red Bull, which Killigrew had frequented as a child, also had a troupe, and William Beeston and his troupe were installed at the Salisbury Court playhouse. Within two months of the Restoration Charles II overrode the existing businesses of these managers. A royal warrant gave the sole right to stage theatrical productions to just two men: William Davenant and Thomas Killigrew. Killigrew had received his reward for entertaining Charles with six years of bawdy jokes. William Davenant had been granted a patent for a theatre back in 1639, and had journeyed to France to petition the future king while he was still in exile. To ensure their monopoly

Thomas Killigrew, the founder of the Theatre Royal, Drury Lane at his desk. He had been a page to Charles I, hence the King's portrait on the wall above him. On his desk is a pile of plays. At his feet sits his dog, wearing a collar with Killigrew's name on it.

was watertight the warrant also ordered all other theatres to be 'absolutely suppressed'. Davenant and Killigrew were to have extra privileges too: they were allowed to censor their own plays, employ women as actors (for the very first time), and by 1663 their licences were made hereditary.

Why did Charles grant only two licences for theatres? A king so fond of entertainment might have been expected to issue many more. The answer is that the theatre was still capable of being politically subversive. In Restoration London violence, civil

disorder and religious dissent bubbled vigorously beneath the surface. Neither Charles, his courtiers, nor business interests wanted
all this stirred up more than necessary. The King, quite simply,
needed to make sure that he could control political and religious
satire in London to prevent it getting out of control. He wanted
theatres to be in the hands of a small number of trusted lieutenants
and to retain the right to censorship. The Master of the Revels,
effectively the royal censor under the Lord Chamberlain's jurisdic-
tion, was paid a fee of 40 shillings to eradicate political and religious
dissent from a proposed play, and ensure that standards of decency
were kept. While this was generally effective in keeping the peace,
it did not stop critical and satirical portrayals of important members
of society from reaching the stage, and if offence was taken revenge
could be waiting down any number of dark alleys.

Killigrew was given a licence to form a company of actors, to be
called the King's Men, and remarkably the present Theatre Royal,
Drury Lane still operates under the same licence. The King's
brother, and successor, James, Duke of York, granted Davenant the
right to a company to be known as the Duke's Men, and the Royal
Opera House, Covent Garden still uses that licence. As their status
became a reality, Davenant and Killigrew must have rubbed their
hands in glee: seven theatres had been built between 1576 and 1605
in a City of 200,000 inhabitants, while in 1660 there were around
300,000 residents in the City, and greater London had 500,000.
The two new theatres could carve up the London theatre audience
between them. Although, over the years, other theatres sprang up,
this monopoly lasted, at least in law, until 1843.

Both Killigrew and Davenant soon opted to convert tennis courts
into theatres. This was probably in response to the fashion for using
indoor tennis courts for theatrical productions in France, to which
Charles and his circle would have been accustomed. By November
Killigrew had already moved a troupe of actors to Gibbons' Tennis
Court in Vere Street, off Oxford Street. It was not very satisfactory:
the stage had no accommodation for scenery and the auditorium
seated only 400. He soon made plans to build a new theatre at
Drury Lane. The capital to do so was raised by selling shares in the

new venture. As a result the ownership of the theatre and its profits were split, causing mismanagement and confusion for more than eighty years, until the arrival of David Garrick. The new building, the first theatre on that site, was completed in May 1663 at a cost of £2,400. Killigrew's new playhouse was fully equipped to deal with scenery and spectacle. However, the whole building was not very large – it probably covered around the same area as the present stage at Drury Lane. It did not last long. On 25 January 1672 the theatre burnt to the ground, taking with it all its scenery, costumes and a good number of surrounding houses and taverns.

Killigrew and his shareholders had to start again, and to finance their second theatre they further complicated ownership by mortgaging the lease of the site and the royal patent. It is not known how much they raised, but the cost of the new theatre has been estimated at somewhere between £3,500 and £4,400. With the finance in place, all Killigrew needed was an architect. We don't know who designed the first theatre but it might have been the architect John Webb, who had built theatres at Whitehall Palace before the Civil War, and again in 1665, but Webb was dead by 1674 and it seems as if Killigrew turned to Christopher Wren. By that date Wren was undisputedly the most famous, successful and fashionable architect in England. Charles II had chosen him to rebuild the royal palace of Whitehall, and had sent him to France to get ideas for his new building. Only a few years later, he had been put in charge of the architectural aspects of the rebuilding of the City of London after the Great Fire of 1666. In 1669 he had received the ultimate accolade when Charles II appointed him Surveyor of the Royal Works, the official royal architect. The key to his career was, as with Killigrew's, royal favour, and this Wren had in spades. Wren and Killigrew must have known each other, though it is doubtful if they could have ever been friends, given Wren's relatively austere and serious-minded character and Killigrew's foppishness. Killigrew's wife Charlotte was the First Lady of the Queen's Privy Chamber, a senior figure in the royal household, and had a substantial lodging at Whitehall: Wren would have undoubtedly known the two of them. It is not known how

Killigrew approached Wren, or what brief he gave him. Perhaps the King himself was consulted, or maybe the three of them discussed the design of theatres generally. Whatever happened, the commission was, without doubt, an exciting one for Wren: he had never had to build a theatre before.

Killigrew must have expected Wren to design him the most modern and fashionable theatre possible, and in doing so both architect and patron must have looked to France. While Charles II was in exile in Paris, Louis XIV allocated him the building we today know as the Palais Royal as his residence (although then it was known as the Palais Cardinal). In it was France's first modern theatre, built in 1635 for Cardinal Richelieu. Charles, and possibly Killigrew too, knew this theatre well; but by 1672 it was very old fashioned, and the theatre that everyone looked to was a building erected in 1659 in the Tuileries, in front of the Louvre. This had been designed by Italian architects on an Italian model, and must have been one of the buildings visited by Christopher Wren when he was in Paris in 1664. Whether Wren bought engravings of the building, whether he sketched it, or even whether he sent for details after being approached by Killigrew we can never know. But what we can be fairly certain of is that Wren used this great French theatre as his model.

We know this because there survives, in Wren's hand, a drawing for the new theatre. It is a section showing the full length of the 112-foot building. To the left are shown the stairs and entrance lobbies on three floors giving entrance to the pit (stalls) and galleries above. To the right of these can be seen the galleries in section, supported by Doric columns. The seats here and in the pit were just benches, without backs, covered in green baize. The centre of the drawing shows an elevation of one wall of the auditorium. Wren shows a perspective effect with six Corinthian pilasters reducing in size towards the stage. Between them are the boxes. The four to the left are in the auditorium and the two on the right are above the stage doors, looking on to the stage itself. Double pilasters mark the archway or opening over the stage, known as the proscenium arch. To the right of this can be seen the scenery in place. At the

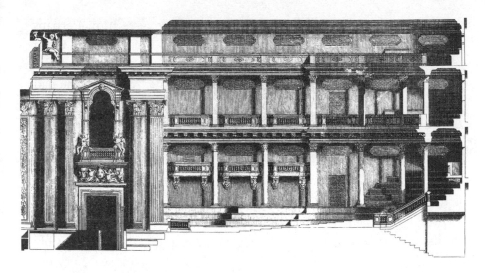

Cross section of the theatre at the Palais des Tuileries in Paris. It was designed by the Italian Gaspare Vigarani for Cardinal Richelieu in 1659. Wren certainly saw this building while he was in Paris in 1665, and it is likely that it was the prototype for the Theatre Royal, Drury Lane.

back of the theatre, on the far right, are the dressing rooms and other offices on the first and second floors, staggered back to make more room at the back of the stage.

Even if this drawing shows the interior of the theatre as built (and we cannot be sure that it was not one of Wren's preliminary drawings), it gives little idea of the site. This was problematic from the very start. The first theatre was completely surrounded by houses and inns, which explains the enormous destruction when it went up in flames. Sir Christopher Wren had to contend with exactly the same problem. The theatre itself was still completely surrounded by other properties and connected to the street only by a narrow passage. What this meant was that the theatre never had an exterior: it had no recognizable street frontage, only a door opening into the long dark passage to the auditorium. It also meant that there could be no side windows. A question therefore is how, without permanent artificial light, could people see inside? The answer may lie in a map of the West End published in 1681–2.

A drawing by Sir Christopher Wren for the Theatre Royal, Drury Lane. This drawing is the only detailed record of the theatre that survives. It may not show the building as built, but be a proposal. However its dimensions fit the site and the interior shown accords with written descriptions and the engraving by William Morgan, overleaf.

This was part of a project started by John Ogilby in 1672 to survey the City and West End and publish a new and comprehensive map of London. His work was under the patronage of both the City of London and Charles II, and was awaited with great eagerness. His map of the West End had small vignettes of important buildings drawn in semi-perspective. One of these is the Drury Lane Theatre, which he shows with a roof similar to that on the Wren drawing but with the addition of a dome, presumably for providing light to the interior. Our problem is that we don't know precisely when Ogilby's surveyors, Gregory King and Robert Felgate, drew their diagram of the theatre. Some people have argued that it shows the first theatre, but it seems as if they were completing their survey at about the time the new theatre was completed – and it would have been madness to publish a map missing out one of the most fashionable new buildings in town. So perhaps the finished building

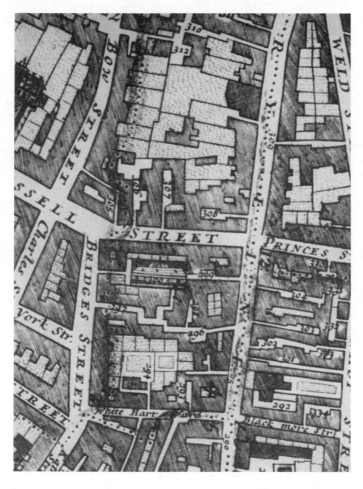

William Morgan's *Prospect of London and Westminster*, published in 1681–2. The detail shows the Theatre Royal, Drury Lane in the centre and to its left the narrow passage that provided access to it from Brydges Street (now Catherine Street). To the right is Drury Lane. Three dormer windows and a hemispherical dome are shown on the roof. The survey work for this map was completed in 1675, the year after the new theatre was completed.

had a small dome on top to provide light to the auditorium. One other chance survival brings the interior of Wren's only theatre to life. An engraving used as a frontispiece to an opera called *Ariadne* almost certainly shows the proscenium arch of the theatre, with

The frontispiece to Pierre Perrin's opera *Ariadne*, performed at the Theatre Royal, Drury Lane in 1674. It shows both the bowed fore-stage in the auditorium and the scenic stage beyond the proscenium arch. In this production no sliding screens were used, just side flats painted with architectural perspective.

great Corinthian pilasters as shown on Wren's drawing. It quite clearly shows the stage and the scenery for the opera, which was performed at the Theatre Royal, Drury Lane in 1674.

Today there are few places that one can go to get an idea of what the Theatre Royal was like when it was finally completed, but a trip to the Theatre Royal in Bristol can get us a long way. Bristol's Theatre Royal was begun in 1764, a hundred years after Wren designed the Theatre Royal, Drury Lane. However Wren's theatre was still in use, albeit altered and redecorated, and was the oldest and most famous theatre in England. The Bristol committee of proprietors, who had bought a site for the new theatre and raised the finance, appointed a Bristol architect, Thomas Patey, to construct their new building. But for a design they looked further afield, to London and to Drury Lane. They employed the Drury Lane carpenter, Mr Sanderson, to give them a design. Sanderson provided a set of designs of Drury Lane in miniature. As a consequence, today in Bristol we can visit a theatre copied directly from Wren's original building. While, scandalously, it had its eighteenth-century stage machinery ripped out in the 1970s, and its stage cut back sometime before that, on its upper balcony it still has benches identical to those on which Samuel Pepys would have sat while watching Nell Gwyn.

The opening of the Theatre Royal in Drury Lane on 26 March 1674 heralded a new era in London theatregoing. There was a world of difference between a converted tennis court and Wren's French-inspired, purpose-designed theatre, equipped with all the latest technology. The gulf between the new building and Elizabethan and Jacobean purpose-built theatres, such as the Globe, was even wider. The new theatre was smaller, it was indoors, and the seats were considerably more expensive. As a consequence it was much more like a wintertime Jacobean performance attended by the better-off and more educated. The incredible social mix of the pre-Commonwealth theatre was to be banished from the world of live entertainment until the twentieth century.

At the pinnacle of the social order was the King himself, and Wren and Killigrew provided a royal box opposite the stage, decorated with bands of leather-gilt trim and a green baize lining, for his use. Charles II was passionate about the stage, and was a frequent member of the Drury Lane audience since plays were performed only rarely at court. His most famous foray into the theatre took place in late 1667. He was in the box with his brother James, Duke of York, and struck up a conversation with a young actress sitting in the next-door box. The royal brothers persuaded her to come and have supper with them afterwards. It was the first of many nights that Charles was to spend with Nell Gwyn, the most famous comedy actress of her day. Nell had been brought up in the theatre and her comedy style was universally admired, almost as much as her breasts and her legs (which sent Samuel Pepys

into ecstasies of admiration). Nell was perhaps Charles's favourite
mistress and her main attraction (apart from a perfect body) was her
unpretentious, coarse wit, something that his aristocratic friends
despised.

Within five years a group of young literati known as the Wits
had gathered around the King. His patronage of the Wits and his
enjoyment of their company made writing for the theatre highly
fashionable among the upper echelons of society and was responsible for drawing more playwrights than at any other time in the
history of the stage from the aristocracy and the gentry. They
incorporated amusing portrayals of each other in their comedies
and they also patronized other, less wealthy, playwrights. The Duke
of Buckingham, the Duke of Newcastle and knights like George
Etherege either wrote or co-wrote plays. Charles himself helped
John Crowne out of playwright's block by suggesting he adapt a
Spanish play, and the resulting *Sir Courtly Nice or It Cannot Be* proved
a great success. Plays were written specifically for the Theatre Royal,
and frequently with particular actors and actresses in mind to play
the lead roles. This created a convention of leading couples sparring
on stage together from production to production. Many actors and
actresses became typecast, whether acting the swarthy villain, the
noble hero, the old maid, the beau, the fop or the rake. For the
first time, actors and actresses became celebrities. Many of the most
famous names of the Restoration stage mean little today, but actors
such as Anne Bracegirdle and Thomas Betterton were household
names in Charles II's London.

Going to the theatre was not an unusual evening out for most of
the audience. It was part of the leisure circuit for rich and fashionable
society – they went frequently, if not several times a week then
several times a month, and they were happy to see the same play
time and again. A seat in the pit cost 2s 6d, in the upper galleries
up to 1s 6d and a seat in one of the boxes 4s. If you had had enough
by the first act you could walk out without paying, or pay less to
come in near the end. Although the season did not continue into
the summer months, there were still around 200 performances a
year. The doors opened at noon but the performance started

between three and four in the afternoon and could go on for another three hours. To avoid having to sit and wait until the show began, or alternatively fight for a seat at the last moment, the well-off paid a servant or a boy to keep a seat until you were ready. In the run-up to the performance orange-sellers plied their trade. Nell Gwyn started her career as an orange-seller working for Mrs Mary Meggs (known as 'Orange Moll'), who had a monopoly on fruit-selling at Drury Lane for thirty-nine years. Oranges were not only refreshment, they were a favourite projectile, to be hurled at the stage or at other members of the audience. Mixing with the orange-sellers were prostitutes touting for clients. Drury Lane was in the red-light district of the West End, and both brothels and streetwalkers were everywhere. Nell's mother may have been a madam, and Nell herself may have worked in her mother's brothel as a child, selling liquid refreshments (only) to clients.

People went to the theatre, as they did to church, to see and be seen. The design of Wren's new theatre made this possible, and large candle-filled chandeliers ensured that the auditorium was as bright as the stage. Prologues, which introduced plays on the first three nights, drew attention to the audience themselves, often satirizing their tastes and dress but also flattering them, particularly those in the more expensive seats. Unlike churchgoers, theatregoers were often rowdy, and their behaviour sometimes degenerated into drunken brawls. Spikes were erected along the edge of the stage at the other London theatre and soldiers were often a looming pres-ence in the auditorium, like modern-day bouncers. The audience chatted and joked through performances, heckling the actors and each other. It was customary for fashionably dressed young Wits to show off with humorous asides or witty interjections as the actors were in mid stride, often on the stage itself. The actors in their turn often played along, giving as good as they got, ensuring an entertaining variety to performances. Nell Gwyn had a famous wit and could reduce the audience to helpless laughter with a fast rejoinder.

No backstage pass was required to gain entry to the dressing rooms and meet the actors and actresses. Fans often invaded the green room (a dressing room covered in green baize), and people were as likely to fall in love with a star as they are today. In October 1667 Mr and Mrs Pepys went to Drury Lane and were taken to the dressing room where Nell Gwyn 'was dressing herself and was all unready'. They may have even visited one of the rooms shown high up behind the stage in Wren's drawing. This glimpse of the actress semi-naked caused Pepys to note that 'she is very pretty, prettier than I thought'. On another occasion Pepys had the chance to kiss her (on the cheek) and was so excited that he mentioned it in his diary twice in one paragraph. Encounters with famous actors could be less happy than this. Stalkers killed the actor William Montfort, jealous of his association with Anne Bracegirdle, whom they attempted to abduct.

Many actresses and some actors became amorously entangled with their patrons, often pursuing affairs with more than one admirer at a time. This had been Nell Gwyn's route to fame: Charles Hart, the manager of Drury Lane and its most famous actor, fell for Nell and gave her the opportunity to go on stage. If the actresses weren't willing to give their attentions to a patron then the prostitutes who plied their trade along with the fruit-sellers in the pit and upper galleries were more than happy to oblige. At this point a box became a useful, if not essential, accessory.

However the Restoration theatre was not simply a bawdy, licentious and rowdy plaything of the aristocracy. The performances were not just incidental background entertainment but were judged by the skill of the actors and the quality of the plays. The audience cheered and clapped at what they liked and booed and jeered at what they didn't. Respectable women from the gentry, such as Pepys' wife, became a regular part of the audience. In the 1670s and 80s these women became a strong pressure group, firstly against raunchy comedy and later in support of tragedy and more civilized comedy. Other less frivolous members of society than fops and gallants frequented the theatre too: men such as the diarist John Evelyn, Judge Jeffreys, the scientist and architect Robert Hooke, and Sir Christopher Wren himself. The social divisions of the house (and to a degree its behaviour) roughly followed seat prices, although these boundaries could always be broken. The cheapest seats, in the gallery, attracted the most derision from satirists. Pepys' outrage at 'citizens, apprentices and others' in the theatre is mainly at their presence in the expensive seats, which annoyed him as much as seeing lowlier work colleagues lording it in better seats than himself.

While we might be able to imagine a Restoration audience, even if we might not want to have been part of one, it is very difficult for us to imagine a Restoration play as it was originally acted. This is partly because no theatre survives today in which the Restoration layout of stage, scenery and seats survives. At Drury Lane the main performance took place on a stage which projected out some 20 feet into the audience in front of the proscenium arch, as shown on the engraving from *Ariadne* and Wren's drawing. This was called the fore-stage. Behind this (in the area that we would normally call the stage today) was the area devoted to scenery – the scenic stage (as it is called). The scenic stage was considerably deeper than the fore-stage, at 45 feet this is clearly seen on Sir Christopher Wren's drawing. It looked even deeper because the scenery was painted in perspective, dwindling to a vanishing point in the centre of the back wall. Scenes were painted on a number of sliding flats either side of the stage and at right angles to it. They were set in grooves in the floor that allowed them to slide either into the wings or out into the stage. Beneath the stage was a complicated system of pulleys and ropes that allowed all the slides to move in or out in unison. The technology was naval, based on the blocks and pulleys used on sailing ships. The only drawback was the noise that changing scenes made, and this was usually covered by sound effects.

This visually and technically complex arrangement could in-stantly reveal spectacular scenes of horrific carnage, victims in the throes of torture or misery, the inside of a prison, tombs or vaults, even heaven and hell. It was also used for revealing or hiding actors, or for the summoning of spirits or deities (who could be called for by stamping a foot). The stage floor contained trap doors, and a system of ropes and pulleys above the stage could allow actors to fly or show clouds opening to reveal gods on chariots. However this setting, with its deep perspective and opportunities to instantly

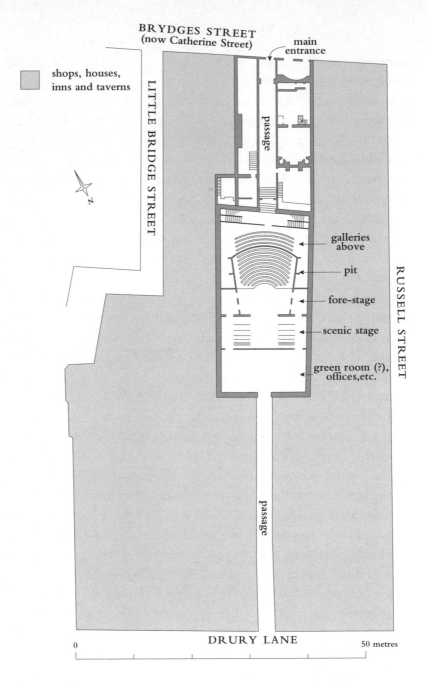

BRYDGES STREET
(now Catherine Street)

main
entrance

shops, houses,
inns and taverns

LITTLE BRIDGE STREET

passage

N

galleries
above

pit

fore-stage

scenic stage

green room (?),
offices, etc.

RUSSELL STREET

passage

0

DRURY LANE

50 metres

No plan of Christopher Wren's Theatre Royal survives, but using his cross section and what we know of the site dimensions it is possible to produce this conjectural plan of the auditorium and stage.

create new scenes, could not accommodate action without de-
stroying the illusion. When characters were discovered behind
shutters they were usually immediately called to the fore-stage if
they were not to look absurd.

Sound effects (partly to conceal the noise of the technology)
were also a common feature of the theatre, and a tradition carried
over from the Elizabethan and Jacobean stage. Drury Lane was
equipped with devices for birdsong (pipes blown into bowls filled
with water), gunfire, cannon blasts, gales and thunder (a cannon ball
rolled down a hollow tree trunk). The fore-stage was illuminated by
hanging rings of burning candles and the scenic stage by rings of
candles hanging behind the proscenium. Sometimes these were
raised and lowered to create the semblance of light and dark. The
system was not very effective. The candles were made of tallow,
that is to say animal fat (mainly from pigs). Burning tallow not only
smelled of burning meat but could give off quite a lot of black
smoke. As the wicks burned down they would need trimming, and
so the chandeliers had to be lowered between acts to allow the
wick-trimmers to do their work. In the summer the intense heat
given off by the hundreds of candles raised the temperature to
intolerable levels. Aside from the smell, the smoke, the trimming
and the heat, if you were unlucky enough to be in the gallery, one
of the chandeliers was almost certain to be obscuring your view.

Acting on the Restoration stage was heavily influenced by the
manners of the day. Actors and actresses wore fashionable clothes,
just like the audience. The Restoration had seen a return to French
styles in dress and manners, which had been common during the
reign of Charles I. These fashions were comprehensively codified
and minutely dissected in books that laid out the correct etiquette
for every situation to achieve maximum grace and decorum.
Fashionable dress could not be divorced from fashionable behaviour, and wearing the latest fashions required considerable attention to deportment and carriage. This inevitably affected the style
of performance on stage by restricting the agility of the actors and
actresses. By the end of the seventeenth century men wore long,
flowing wigs with deep, turbulent curls topped with a plumed hat.

Lace, gold and silver embroidery, rouged cheeks and beauty spots were as important for men as they were for women. Men wore coloured high-heeled ankle boots, sometimes garnished with ribbons. Their stockinged calves were on full display, and by the last decade of the century they wore elaborately decorated coats, fitted at the waist, with baggy pockets hanging around their breeches. Lace bloomed from their wrists and necks, and trimmed their shirts. Their sleeves were wide and floppy, offset by a dangling sword and a cane.

Women were shaped by tight-fitted wooden or bone corsets that pulled in their waists and accentuated their breasts, constricting their movements. When out in public they wore a train. This had to be delicately manoeuvred, and their voluminous skirts would have continually knocked against their high-heeled shoes as they walked; sitting too became a subtle art. Elaborate hairstyles were often made up with ribbons and topped with a hood. To complete the look, fans and masks were used to dramatic effect. However, one of the reasons female actors caused such a sensation on the Restoration stage was the possibility of seeing them in 'breeches parts'. In these roles women dressed as men, to much hilarity, to test their suitors, and were usually discovered by having their hats and wigs whipped off to reveal their long, cascading hair. What was particularly appealing and risqué about breeches parts was that they were the only opportunity for women to show off their legs, or as much of their bodies as men's clothes allowed, in public. The popularity of the roles can be seen in the extent to which they were performed on the stage: 89 of the 375 plays staged between 1660 and 1700 had one or more breeches parts. When Nell Gwyn played a famous breeches part in a play called *The Mad Couple*, Charles Sackville, Lord Buckhurst, the Restoration's most famous and outrageous rake, was so inflamed by the sight of her rolling around on the stage in her breeches that he took her as his mistress.

Costumes were extremely valuable and actors who were tempted to take their fancy clothes out of the theatre faced losing a week's wages. Stage dress often came in the form of donations from the court or rich patrons: Charles's coronation robe was one of the features at Drury Lane, while other donations included wedding gowns or suits. A convention developed to protect costumes from excessive wear and tear by staging death scenes on a green cloth, where death throes could take place without damaging fine laces or fabrics. Historical costume, if used, was usually combined with the fashions of the day, so that togas were juxtaposed with wigs, and similar bizarre combinations were employed for plays set in faraway lands.

Acting itself was highly stylized, indeed wooden by modern standards. Comedy acting was the most 'realistic', exaggerating behaviour that the audience would have considered normal. Yet this was still very stylized because of the nature of the characters which the actors were playing. Stock personalities with obviously identifiable traits were easily recognizable and understood by the audience. Stock expressions were also employed to portray common emotional states. In tragedy this was more pronounced. The tragic style was considered a higher art and more difficult to master: it was more formal and closely related to the art of rhetoric (public speaking) used by lawyers and preachers. Physically much of the action focused on hands creating melodramatic gestures, though exaggerated facial expressions were important too. Gestures and expressions may have imitated reality to an extent, but were more often symbolic. Next most important was the delivery of the lines themselves, or the tone of voice used to deliver them. In Drury Lane the actors were very close to their audience – the back of the auditorium was only 32 feet away – and while they would have had to project their voices, much of their characterization would have been expressed through tone rather than in a booming declaration. The special praise bestowed on actors and actresses for remaining in character while other actors were speaking during this period suggests that it was rare to do so and far more common to simply switch off.

Despite the fame of the Theatre Royal, Drury Lane, its scenery, costumes and actors, it was a very unstable business venture. Disputes between actors, managers and patentees over pay and procedure became commonplace. These resulted in walk-outs; the departure of key staff and actors to other theatres; and even the intervention of the Lord Chamberlain to close the theatre and restore order. It was not until the arrival of David Garrick as manager at Drury Lane in 1747 that it became anything like a solid business interest.

Garrick, of French Huguenot extraction, was born in Hereford in 1717 and brought up in Lichfield. His grandfather, David Garric, escaped to England with his family, having feared Catholic persecution in his native Bordeaux, where he had a successful wine business. His father, Pierre, now Peter Garrick, managed to buy a commission in the Army and marry into the Church by wedding the daughter of one of the vicars choral at Lichfield Cathedral. Thus although David Garrick came from a respectable family they were by no means well off, and their future was never certain. David's early ability to entertain through mimicry drew the attention of a wealthy neighbour, Gilbert Walmesley, who was at the centre of the cultural and intellectual life of Lichfield. With no children of his own he became keenly involved in the interests of bright young boys with little financial means. Through Walmesley Garrick met his lifelong friend and senior by eight years, Samuel Johnson. On 2 March 1737 these two young men, soon to dominate the worlds of the theatre and literature, left Lichfield for the capital, 120 miles away, with a few pennies and one horse between them. One rode the horse for a distance, then tied it up for the other to collect and walked on, and in this way they reached London. Within a week Garrick enrolled at the Inns of Court to study law. However on 19 March his father died. This was a disaster because his father had not yet sold his commission in the Army, leaving the family without any capital. His elder brother Peter came up with the plan that David should quit his studies and go into the wine trade with him, with their uncle providing financial backing.

The Garricks chose Durham Yard off the Strand for their wine business. This was within easy reach of the theatres in Drury Lane and Covent Garden, and David immediately made friends of actors and managers in the local coffee houses and gained access to the green rooms of the theatres. From an early age Garrick had been interested in the theatre and would have seen many of the touring plays that came through Lichfield. In 1727, only ten years old, he produced Farquhar's *The Recruiting Officer* in the great hall of the bishop's palace. He took complete control of auditions, costume and set, putting his sister Jenny in the part of Lucy and himself in the lead comic role of Sergeant Kite. As far as actually becoming an actor was concerned, Garrick had to tread very carefully. He was aware of the potentially devastating effect that such a move would cause in family relations, especially with his uncle. Acting was considered socially unacceptable for the son of an officer and a gentleman, and so Garrick was forced to settle for amateur dramatics at the home of the painter and publisher Edward Cave, where in 1739 he staged Fielding's *The Mock Doctor* and starred in the leading role. But as it became increasingly obvious that his wine business was doomed to failure, Garrick decided to try out his luck on the stage.

In 1741 Garrick had his first real break when Henry Gifford, the manager of Goodman's Fields (an unlicensed theatre just outside the boundaries of the City and Westminster), gave him the chance to make his first proper entrance as understudy for an actor who had fallen ill. This was in *Harlequin Student*, a mime play, and as the part was masked Garrick was able to keep his identity concealed. That summer Gifford took his company on tour to Ipswich and allowed Garrick to join him, but his real chance came in October 1741 when Gifford agreed to let him perform the lead role in *Richard III* at Goodman's Fields. This version of Shakespeare's *Richard III* had previously been the sole property of the famous early eighteenth-century actor Colley Cibber, but with his retirement the prominent actor James Quin managed to gain almost sole rights to it. So by choosing *Richard III* Garrick took a part which the theatregoing public knew almost by heart, and which had been performed by the most famous actors of the day. One of their favourite lines, which they waited for with great anticipation, came when Richard heard news of Buckingham's arrest: 'Off with his head! So much for Buckingham.' The other was the line delivered after his nightmare: 'Conscience avaunt! Richard is himself again.'

It was by his delivery of famous lines like these at key moments that Garrick knew he was going to be judged.

The poster advertising the play declared the part of King Richard would be played by 'a Gentleman (who never appeared on any stage)'. This was common practice for newcomers and meant that they could retire if they proved a failure without too much shame. On 19 October 1741 the five foot, three inch aspiring actor walked out on to the stage to perform to an audience that included some of his closest friends. It was an enormous success. The next day the *London Daily Post and General Advertiser* described his reception as 'the most extraordinary and great that was ever known on such an occasion'.

Word-of-mouth spread the news that at Goodman's Fields a sensation was to be seen. People queued for tickets and the roads were clogged with coaches making their way east to see the new talent. Garrick quickly wrote to his brother, informing him of his decision to leave the wine business before they both went bankrupt. He also noted that in his new profession he could earn as much as £300 a year, the traditional income of a gentleman. It was Garrick's anxious experience of the wine business and his time under Gifford which were later to establish him as the greatest actor-manager of the eighteenth century and to ensure that Drury Lane became London's and the nation's premier theatre.

What spectators raved about was Garrick's great acting ability, particularly his astonishing interpretation of character. This was his 'natural' style – considered at the time to be a spine-chilling or heart-wrenching portrayal of nature or reality; certainly not what we would consider realism. It was realistic only in comparison to the formalized style of the Restoration, where actors had portrayed universal types such as villain, hero or coward with formulaic gestures and emotional responses. Theatre critics had for some time been praising a new style of acting which not only took into consideration the universal types but also brought out the individual character of a role. The burly Irish actor Charles Macklin, who later killed a fellow actor in a brawl, had caused a stir with his sympathetic and fierce portrayal of Shylock in *The Merchant of Venice* in 1741. Shylock had previously been portrayed as a simple stock character, but spectators were mesmerized by Macklin's portrayal of Shylock's disintegration, demonstrated by his increasingly unkempt hair and clothing. His inspiration was based on careful research and the observation of elderly Jews in London's coffee houses. It was Macklin who coached the young Garrick, and the role of Richard III had never been performed with such a degree of realism. The two lines which audiences waited for allowed Garrick to use his skills to the full, going through an extraordinary visual transformation of mood from one sentiment to another. This was the age of the dramatic pause, when actors would freeze in a specific arresting pose at a poignant moment.

The moment that came to define Garrick's portrayal of Richard III is of the tent scene, when Garrick stood with the fingers of his right hand extended, a startled look on his face and his other hand reaching for a dagger – as captured in Hogarth's famous painting of Garrick, now in the Walker Art Gallery Liverpool (see Plate 6). Before the days of photography spectators remembered particular gestures, movements and facial expressions and came to expect the exact same performance the next time. The precise tableau of a scene on stage would be discussed in coffee houses and taverns, just like a painting. These expectations bred conservatism, since audiences expected to see the familiar *Richard III* rather than some innovation.

Garrick managed to deliver 169 performances, taking eighteen different parts by the spring of 1742. In his first season at Goodman's Fields he earned his £300, and eventually 50 per cent of the box office receipts too. Garrick then played at all the major theatres in London, and just before departing to Smock Alley Theatre in Dublin for the summer season of 1742 he played at Drury Lane in three different roles, earning the sum of £400. This won him an agreement to act at Drury Lane in the following season for £500 and a share of the box office. He was now on the same salary as James Quin, who had been on the stage for forty years.

During his first few seasons at Drury Lane Garrick experienced the same fights and walkouts over pay that had persistently dogged the running of the company, and was involved in an unsuccessful walkout which led to a public falling-out with Macklin. In 1747 he entered into partnership with the Irish actor James Lacy for the management of Drury Lane, buying a half share in the theatre's patent for £8,000. He agreed to act exclusively at Drury Lane, receiving 500 guineas as an actor and £500 as manager each year, and taking the sole rights over all matters concerning the stage, including the hiring of actors, while Lacy was allowed to make decisions along with Garrick over pay. Garrick also stipulated that his brother George be given the running of the theatre's office, and he named his solicitor as arbitrator should disputes arise.

Two formidable actors were already at Drury Lane: Spranger Barry, singled out for his Othello, and the all-round actor and playwright Thomas Mozeen. Garrick realized that the Theatre Royal would rise or fall on the quality of its actors. He moved quickly to poach some of the finest talents from his greatest competitor, John Rich at Covent Garden. He took to Drury Lane the well-known performers William Harvard, Mrs Cibber and Mrs Pritchard. Garrick's enthusiasm for his new role as actor-manager and his concern for the box office meant that he performed far more regularly himself than when he was a mere actor. In his first season he made 165 appearances on the stage, compared to an average of sixty-five before. Of the thirty-one benefit nights, he appeared in thirteen, including one for the benefit of victims of a fire in Cornhill, and appeared in eighteen more the following season. He also acted in thirteen roles. Altogether the company put on 172 nights of performances, twenty more than the previous season and a far greater number than Covent Garden, which only succeeded in putting on 104.

The theatregoing public comprised a far greater spectrum than in the Restoration theatre. Audiences were drawn from all parts of society: members of parliament; lawyers and students from the Inns of Court; apprentices, merchants and tradesmen; those visiting London, such as ambassadors and rich tourists; the investors in shares, who benefited from free seats; the actors' friends and family; along with journalists and critics. Boxes cost 5 shillings a seat and were usually filled with the nobility or wealthy members of the gentry; a seat on a bench in the pit, where the gentry would have rubbed shoulders with critics and intellectuals, cost 3 shillings; the lower gallery cost 2 shillings and was filled with freemen; whilst the upper gallery cost 1 shilling and was filled with the less wealthy footmen, sailors and apprentices. In terms of noise and nuisance, Garrick's theatre was very similar to that of the Restoration. In 1755 Garrick brought Jean Noverre to Drury Lane, one of the greatest figures in French ballet history. He was to perform *Les Fêtes Chinoises*, which Garrick billed as the *Chinese Festival*. His timing was bad. Britain was on the brink of war with France and anti-French feelings were running high. Garrick, aware that there could be protests, went out of his way to advertise the fact that Noverre was not only Swiss but a Protestant too. On the first night the performance was booed, despite the fact that George II himself was in the theatre. On the following nights angry disturbances in the audience made the show unintelligible. On the Saturday night the disaffection exploded. Seats were torn up, mirrors and chandeliers smashed, the stage was stormed, and the audience was only driven away by staff wielding cudgels.

Despite these occasional riots, Garrick's skilful management and hard work led the theatre into substantial profit: it yielded over £6,000 annually. Within a couple of years Garrick was rich by the standards of the day. His personal profits and fees were somewhere in the region of £5,000 a year. In 1749 he proposed to the Catholic dancer Violette or Eva-Maria Veigel and they were wed on 22 June in both a Catholic and a Protestant ceremony. She brought with her a dowry of £5,000 a year from a benefactor and Garrick gave her a lump sum of £10,000 and £70 annually. They bought a house within walking distance of Drury Lane at 27 Southampton Street, where they lived for the next twenty-three years.

Garrick started his management by giving the theatre a minor refurbishment in the form of a lick of paint and an increase in seating to bring in an extra £40 a night. He also forced theatregoers to pay at the box office on entry, an unpopular move. But more important were Garrick's innovations to the stage and in the management of plays and of actors. His company was made up of sixty-eight performers – actors, singers and dancers. Fifty staff were also employed to run the theatre. This complement required that general meetings took place in the green room, a common room situated to the side of the stage. Soon a communication system was set up whereby grievances were written down and resolved by management. Messages were posted to three main areas: for those working in the theatre it was the prompter's office; for authors it was the Bedford Coffee House; and for tradesmen it was the offices of Lacy, Pritchard and George Garrick. This was Garrick's attempt to centralize the company and to stop disputes escalating into walkouts or strikes. For the business side he used the advice of merchants, lawyers and bankers outside his company, while he consulted actors within the company for matters of production and management. Garrick also put a heavy emphasis on rehearsal, making it compulsory for all: previously it had frequently been an optional extra.

On stage he departed from the traditional scenes with a standard vanishing point and produced vivid pieces of scenery that the actors could walk in and around without spoiling the perspective effect. He used colour transparencies that created dramatic colour changes: leaves could change in magical gardens, fiery lakes and waterfalls could be created instantly. This was a further move towards 'naturalism', creating fantastic worlds that appeared more real. Between 1765 and 1766 he removed the chandelier above the fore-stage and incorporated new footlights along with oil lamps in the wings. Shortly before he retired he made two further significant changes. The first was the employment, in 1771, of Philip de Loutherbourg, an Alsatian painter, set designer and lighting technician. His role was not only to create new set designs and organize stage machinery, but also to coordinate lighting and costume. He was required to produce spectacular sets with exciting effects each winter, and worked to create these through the summer. For the 1774–5 season he transformed the staging of *The Maid of Oaks*, a slightly tepid comedy of manners, into a spectacle. The culmination was a scene reproducing a great outdoor entertainment, including views of the house at which it was held, and gardens complete with statues, temples and realistic rays from the sun. The scenery alone cost £1,500. In all De Loutherbourg worked on around fifteen sets in the four years until Garrick's retirement.

Garrick's partner John Lacy died in January 1774, leaving Garrick in sole control of the theatre. His own thoughts were turning to retirement, but before he went, he decided to embark on one last project – the modernization of Wren's 100-year-old theatre. This was long overdue. Not only was the auditorium old fashioned and uncomfortable, but the theatre had grown piecemeal over the previous century. With the many additions made over the years, it now covered some 13,134 square feet and included nine other buildings attached to the main theatre. These housed subsidiary functions such as joinery, painting, the wardrobe, a scenery room, and business and administrative offices for the treasurers, prompters and box attendants. There were also dozens of rooms used for dressing and rehearsals along with a library where actors kept their scripts, a room for music scores and a copying room. Despite these additions the great theatre still had no street frontage, and people still entered through a passage.

Garrick wanted to rationalize and aggrandize his theatre, and he needed an architect to help him realize his dream. His search for an architect was as simple as Killigrew's a hundred years before. He turned to London's most fashionable architect, Robert Adam. Adam had come to London from his native Scotland in 1758 with his brother James. Already a talented architect, he immediately moved into the fashionable circle of artists that was inhabited by talents like Sir Joshua Reynolds and Garrick himself. Garrick soon became a friend, client, business partner and eventually neighbour of the brothers. In the mid 1760s the Adams launched an incredibly ambitious and financially risky luxury housing development just off the Strand, on what are now Adam and John Adam Streets. It was to be called the Adelphi (meaning 'brothers' in Greek). Garrick agreed to rent one of these super-fashionable houses when they were completed in 1772, and lived there in a house close to Robert's for the last six years of his life. Thus not only fashion but also friendship led to Garrick's choice of Adam, and the two men must have carefully considered all the aspects of the theatre's redesign together.

First of all they gave the theatre a street frontage by building a frontispiece on Brydges Street – a magnificent stucco-fronted façade with a rusticated basement and elegant Ionic columns supporting a pediment proudly containing the royal arms. No one could be in any doubt that behind this elegant façade lay a place of real quality and style. Inside Adam dismantled Wren's interior, enlarging the size of the auditorium and the stage at the expense of some of the subsidiary offices. He removed the heavy pilasters that had always restricted views of the stage and replaced them with slender square columns. The wooden faces of the balconies and other timber elements were decorated with typical Adam motifs in composition plaster. The general effect of these modifications can be gained by a visit to any house by Adam – Kenwood House in Hampstead, for instance. The ceiling was raised and painted in *trompe l'œil* to represent a shallow dome (see Plate 7). Was this an echo of the dome that Wren may have originally crowned his theatre with?

There was one particularly remarkable innovation. The square pillars that supported the balconies were faced with sheets of glass laid over spangled foils, coloured crimson on the lower tier and green on the upper. The capitals of these spangled pillars were gold, giving a very striking effect. This was a new technique developed by Adam while he was working for the Duke of Northumberland. Garrick, always interested in innovation, wanted to invest in it.

The Duke of Northumberland wanted to produce sheets of plate glass large enough to adorn the interiors that Adam was designing for his houses. Until that time the only source of large sheets of plate glass was France. In 1773 Adam and Garrick invested the enormous sum of £12,000 in a plate glass factory in Lancashire. The venture was slow to produce results and neither the Theatre Royal nor Northumberland's drawing room were to benefit from English glass. Perhaps they were never meant to. Garrick was a canny businessman and perhaps believed that by introducing glass pilasters into his theatre he might trigger a trend, thus creating

1. This is a detail from a painting in the Royal Collection at Hampton Court called *The Family of Henry VIII*. It shows a glimpse over the privy garden at Whitehall looking towards one of the decorated southern wings of the palace. A servant is seen in the garden near the low shin-rails and beasts on poles.

2. William Beckford painted by George Romney.

3. A watercolour by J. M. W. Turner showing Fonthill Abbey in *c.*1797. The top of the tower was, at this stage, closely modelled on the mausoleum of King John at Batalha in Portugal.

4. John Rutter's view of St Michael's Gallery, 1823. This clearly shows Beckford's collections in cabinets and the bookcases with their curtains.

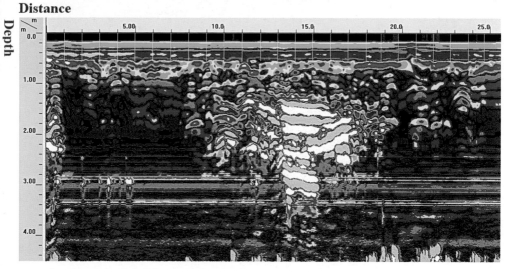

5. Radargram from a ground-penetrating radar showing the foundations of the central tower of Fonthill Abbey in section. Ground level is the black layer at the top; the red is soil; the pale shape in the centre the foundation. At this point it was 3.5 metres deep.

6. William Hogarth's portrait of Garrick as Richard III, painted in 1745.

Design of a Ceiling for the Theatre Royal in Drury Lane.

Adelphi July 19th 1775.

Scales of 1 2 3 4 5 6 7 8 9 10 15 20 Feet

7. Robert Adam's original coloured design for a new ceiling for the Theatre Royal, Drury Lane, drawn in 1775.

8. This fourteenth-century illuminated manuscript shows a siege under way at a castle. The attackers are attempting to storm the walls using ladders under cover of archers and engineers using a perrier, a type of mangonel.

9. A fourteenth-century illuminated manuscript showing miners starting to dig a mine beneath the walls of a castle. They are sheltering under a wheeled cover while the defenders throw great stakes, boulders and fire from the battlements above.

10. The fire that destroyed the ducal palace at Nottingham in 1831 was recorded by a number of artists including this anonymous one. The fire finally saw the end of the castle site as a symbol of power and authority and ushered in its more democratic use as a public park and art gallery.

11. An early photograph showing the great rusticated gate of Millbank Penitentiary.

12. The ruins of Glastonbury Abbey from the south. In the foreground is the abbot's kitchen and in the background, behind the ruined walls of the abbey church, is the town of Glastonbury and St Michael's parish church.

The elegant stucco façade of the Theatre Royal, Drury Lane that
finally, in 1775, replaced an unassuming door as the entrance to the
theatre. Commissioned by David Garrick and designed by Robert
Adam, it was intended to herald the sophistication and elegance of
the theatre within.

Engraving of the interior of the Theatre Royal, Drury Lane after Robert Adam refitted it for David Garrick in 1775. The view is taken from the stage and shows the square columns decorated with sparkling glass that supported the balconies. The balcony fronts are decorated in typical Adam style with plasterwork. The ceiling is painted in imitation of a dome.

demand for the new factory. Most people were impressed by the glittering interior of the Theatre Royal, but the glass panels were removed in 1783 and Adam's glittery glass interiors became a footnote in the history of eighteenth-century interior design and not the money-spinner that he had hoped. Nevertheless parts of the drawing room of Northumberland House still exist and can be seen in the British Galleries at the Victoria and Albert Museum. They presumably formed the inspiration for the manufacture of glitter plastic in the 1970s.

The transformation of the Theatre Royal was Garrick's last contribution to the English stage, and all that was left for him was to retire in the glory he deserved. But first he needed to sell off his share in the theatre patent, the value of which had now risen to £35,000. He completed the sale in June, after six months of negotiations, to Richard Brinsley Sheridan, Thomas Linley and Richard Ford. As the secret negotiations were under way the press got wind of his intention to sell up and retire. A social frenzy resulted. Everyone wanted to be at one of the farewell performances – tickets had never been hotter. Between 7 March and 10 June Garrick performed the most successful roles of his career, including Hamlet, King Lear and Richard III. On his last night he ended his 35-year career as Don Felix in the comedy, *The Wonder*. The house had been packed for three months: duchesses were forced to beg for tickets and sit where they could with ladies of the lowest station. At the end of his last performance Garrick approached the audience and, visibly moved, was just able to make a bow. He then delivered his final farewell speech, telling his fans, 'This is to me a very awful moment; it is no less than parting for ever from those from whom I have received the greatest kindness, and those favours were enjoyed.' Choked with emotion, he took his final bow and left the stage to the cheers and tears of a packed house. Even after retirement Garrick was still involved in the theatre and helped Sheridan with the revision of a number of Restoration plays; he even directed Sheridan's *School for Scandal* in 1777. In July 1778 his health deteriorated and he died on 20 January 1779 at the Adelphi. On 1 February his body was driven at the head of a procession of fifty carriages to Westminster Abbey, where he was interred close to Shakespeare's monument.

Thus was laid to rest one of the great eighteenth-century polymaths. Over two hundred portraits, drawings and prints were made of him by the most famous painters of the day, including William Hogarth, Sir Joshua Reynolds and Sir Thomas Gainsborough. He was an actor, director, author, manager, businessman, and a man of wit and taste who remained at the top of his profession for thirty-five years. He was, in modern terms, a multimillionaire with an amazing collection of paintings and sculptures, which he left to the British Museum. It is not really possible to find a modern equivalent of such a man. And his career was made possible by a building, itself no ordinary structure. Drury Lane was Britain's first modern theatre, a building that became a laboratory for the experiments that created theatre as we know it. It is unbelievable that a building of such importance could have been torn down, but it was.

Wren's theatre was demolished in 1791 and rebuilt three years later to make way for an enormous auditorium with a seating capacity of 3,611. In the hope of bringing back the Messiah, a deranged soldier tried to shoot George III there as he blew a kiss to his subjects from his royal box, missing him by inches. The world's most famous clown, Joe Grimaldi, Master Betty the child star, Carlo the Dog and Edmund Kean all trod the new theatre's boards. But in 1809 Sheridan watched as it burnt to the ground. Asked why he appeared so calm, he declared, 'Cannot a man take a glass of wine by his own fireside?' The present theatre is the fourth on the site, built in 1812 to hold 3,060 and modified in 1922 to seat 2,226.

Not a single trace of the original theatre survives beneath the present imposing building. Yet performances proudly continue under the original patent issued by King Charles. That patent triggered a sequence of events that saw a single building give birth to a whole theatrical tradition. As it did, it made London the theatre capital of the world. Each night as the doors of London's theatres disgorge thousands of satisfied theatregoers they have reason to thank the influence of one of Britain's great lost buildings for a fine night out.

Nottingham Castle
Architecture as Tyranny

Of all the lost buildings of England, none has been so successfully erased from our sight as Nottingham Castle. Once one of the largest, most luxurious and best-defended castles in England, it is now nothing more than a few disconnected stones. Despite its extraordinary impregnability, Nottingham was not a castle solely built for military action: its purpose was both cruder and subtler. It was quite simply a symbol of royal might and oppression. As such it has attracted men who wanted to dominate and oppress their fellows as well as those who wanted to rise up against authority. The history of Nottingham Castle is the story of a very great building, but it is also the story of the struggle of men to be free from tyranny.

Nottingham Castle was founded by William the Conqueror on his way to York in the winter of 1067–8. It was an obvious place to build a castle. Nottingham was a crossing point on the river Trent (which was navigable up to the town, making Nottingham a port) and lay on the main route to York from central England. Securing this strategic town and intimidating its population must have been a priority for the Norman invaders, especially as it was a superb defensive site. To the west of the old English town is a narrow sandstone crag with steep cliffs on one side, rising to 60 metres (200 feet) above sea level. At its foot was the river Leen (now dried up), a tributary of the Trent, diverted from its course to form a southern defence, and from its summit huge swathes of Nottinghamshire are visible. A finer site for a great castle could hardly be imagined.

The first castle, built at speed and in timber, was typical of its age. It was based on a series of concentric rings of defence, ensuring that if one line was broken there was another to be held. Most castles of the period were built with two enclosures or wards, one containing a motte or hill where the inner residential parts were located, and the second, larger outer ward for the household and soldiers. At Nottingham, by the late twelfth century, there were actually three wards. On the highest part of the rock, perched on the sheer cliff top, was a natural motte forming the inner ward; the middle ward occupied the rest of the higher land; and a large outer ward enclosed arable land, ponds and mills below. To the west there was a large royal hunting park.

The invading Norman army built a network of such castles across England to secure the country from rebellion and provide fortified power bases in an incredibly unstable and violent society. Yet it would be a mistake to regard Nottingham Castle or any of the other castles of Norman England as purely military buildings. They were residences centred on huge landholdings, bridgeheads for ruling the country, and the social, economic and administrative hubs of their regions. Both town dwellers and peasants in their villages would regard the local castle as the most visible symbol of authority and government in their lives. For this reason, just as much as any defensive one, castles needed to look mighty and use the architectural language of warfare. This was especially important for the king's castles, which also symbolized royal dominance over the nobility and thus had to be supreme in scale and strength. For all these reasons the Norman and early Plantagenet years were dominated architecturally by castle-building.

Castles were costly, and royal castles extremely so. It was possible to build a very basic castle for £350, but most castles of the nobility cost around £1,000. However the improvements to the imposing and impenetrable royal castle at Dover, between 1180 and 1190, cost £7,000. The sheer expense of castle-building always put the king at an advantage over his subjects. The average annual revenue of a Norman baron in the twelfth century was £200, and only seven of them enjoyed an income of more than £400; more than twenty of them had to make do with less than £20. The king massively outstripped them with an income of about £10,000 a year. Of this vast fortune by far the greatest single expenditure, accounting for between 7 and 10 per cent of royal income, was castle-building. This haemorrhage of royal resources was crucial both to secure the borders of England and to create centres of royal government and power. Unlike Dover, Newcastle or Bristol, all of which were border defences, Nottingham was principally a centre for royal authority. It was a residence, a seat of administration, a prison, a courtroom, a treasury and, of course, a fortress.

The Norman kings lived an itinerant life, ceaselessly travelling the country and staying briefly in royal and baronial castles as well as smaller hunting lodges as they went. They were followed by a host of servants, soldiers and officials who serviced both their domestic requirements and the administration necessary to rule. The Norman royal household on the road would have been a very impressive sight, with the king and his barons in their finery riding at the head of an enormous and unwieldy baggage train. Royal castles, like Nottingham, had to have sufficient accommodation not only for the king and queen (if she accompanied him) but for this enormous royal entourage. There would be very little permanent furniture in a royal castle, perhaps only the basic tables and benches: all the king's personal possessions, from his cutlery to his bed, would be brought in and set up just in advance of his arrival. The castle was like a stage set and had to be dressed each time the royal household arrived. Kings of England frequently visited Nottingham. Henry II, the first of the Plantagenets, who rebuilt the castle, stayed there seven times between 1155 and 1185, celebrating Christmas there in 1180 and summoning Parliament to it three times. On these occasions the castle was the focus for glittering royal ceremonial and national events. Most of the time, however, it was largely empty under the custodianship of its constable, usually a member of the local gentry, and a respected and well-off servant of the Crown. He would have had a skeleton staff including a few servants, a porter at the gate, some watchmen, gamekeepers in the park, and probably a chaplain. It was his task to keep the castle well maintained, to exercise royal legal authority in the locality, and prepare the castle for royal use.

The timber fortresses of the early Norman period gradually became obsolete as military technology advanced. One by one the timber ramparts of the Conqueror's castles were replaced in stone. The first stone structure built at Nottingham was a tall tower (normally known as a keep), built on the motte and visible for miles around. Then between 1170 and 1188 everything apart from the outer ward was rebuilt in stone by Henry II at a cost of £1,800. While William the Conqueror's first castle would have been built by forced labour under the direction of Norman carpenters, professional masons constructed Henry II's castle. Stone was brought across country from Northamptonshire and wood cut from nearby Sherwood Forest. The King's engineers, based in Westminster, would have supervised the whole operation, and hundreds of craftsmen would have descended on the town while building work was under way. What they constructed for Henry II was no ordinary castle. It was exceptionally well appointed – indeed it could be counted, together with Windsor and Winchester, as a palace-fortress, one of the most luxurious and comfortable residences in the kingdom.

The inner ward of the castle, the most secure part, contained the royal accommodation. It was entered by its own fortified gatehouse from the middle ward and was dominated by the keep, a 40 foot square tower containing two floors of rooms reserved for the most important royal ceremonial. Below, entered by a separate door, was a dark dungeon. Round the battlemented walls of the inner ward were the monarch's residential apartments. The King's apartments were next to the keep and comprised three rooms: an outer waiting room, a reception chamber and a bedchamber. Off this, probably in the keep, was his private chapel, dedicated to St Nicholas. The King's rooms would have been very simple, probably thatched, with unglazed windows with wooden shutters looking inwards to the courtyard. The outer two rooms would have been sparsely furnished, perhaps with some tables, benches and stools. The walls were probably painted white with simple repeated decorative motifs such as roses or fleurs-de-lis in red or yellow. The royal bedchamber would have contained a bed in a curtained enclosure. Around this, on the floor, would have slept the King's inner household and companions. Attached to the bed-chamber would have been a garderobe or privy for royal use. Even the King had to make do with a glorified plank with a hole in its centre. When he relieved himself he may have been sitting over the edge of the cliff – no wonder a euphemism for lavatory was 'draught'. If the King wished he could dine in his lodgings, served from his own private kitchen and bakehouse and supplied from his own cellars. On the other side of the inner ward from the King's rooms was a suite of rooms for the Queen. They would have been similarly furnished, and contained a chapel known as the White Chapel, as well as a wardrobe. Between the two, surrounded by covered walkways, was a herb garden for the King and Queen to walk in.

In the middle ward were the stables, kitchens and great hall. The hall built by Henry II in 1181–3 was the largest single building in the castle and its social and symbolic heart. It was a massive aisled building with a log fire burning on a hearth in its centre. Smoke from this found its way upwards to the rafters and out of a louvre (or vent) in the roof. At one end, on a slightly raised platform, was the King's table. Beneath him tables laid out along the length of the hall would have accommodated the most important people in his household. Eating in here, supplied from a kitchen sited at the far end from the King, would be a daily event. The hall was also home to entertainment in the evening, and when the King wished to conduct a large assembly of dignitaries the hall would serve for that too. For many of his household, at night it would be their bedroom. Straw mattresses would be pulled out from storage and laid on the floor. The lucky ones would be near the central fire, the servants would shiver on the periphery. Both men and women would sleep together in here amidst hunting dogs sniffing around in the straw laid on the floor. The other major structure in the middle ward was a chapel, served by the full-time castle chaplain. The household and garrison would have attended a service in here every day, and the King himself would attend on Sunday and feast days.

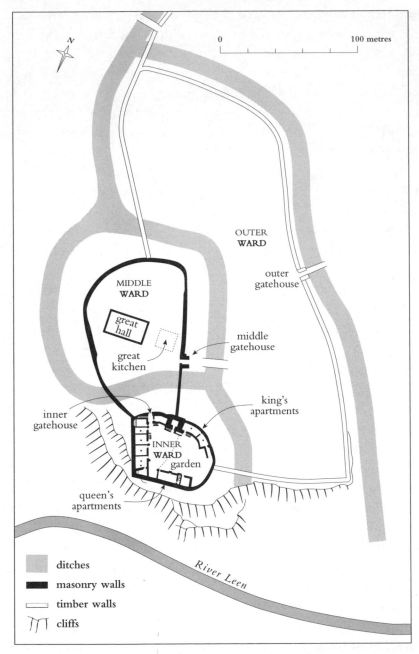

Nottingham Castle in the time of Richard I. The location of many of the buildings in the middle ward is unknown. The great hall has been located by archaeological excavation.

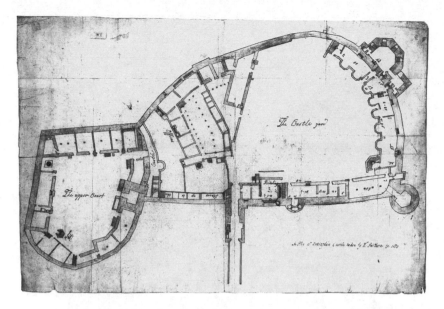

Plan of Nottingham Castle made in 1617 by the surveyor and architect John Smythson. This is the only surviving plan of the castle and the principal source of evidence for it. Sadly many of the original medieval buildings had already been demolished before Smythson's survey was made.

The horses used to pull the wagons and carts of the royal baggage train would probably be put out to graze in the outer ward, but the King's own horses and those of his barons were carefully tended and groomed in stables sited in the middle ward. Nearby there was also a hawk mews for the King's hunting birds, and probably kennels for his dogs. Also in the middle ward were storerooms for food and military provisions; workshops for masons, carpenters and blacksmiths; and lodgings for the garrison. If the castle had to be reinforced many of the extra troops would be billeted in the outer ward, in tents.

It is difficult to visualize this early castle: most castles of that date have either been destroyed or much altered and extended over successive centuries. But a visit to Peveril Castle in the Peak District can give us an idea. Like Nottingham it is precariously perched on a stone outcrop and surrounded by what are technically known as

Although the keep at Nottingham does not survive, that at Peveril Castle in Derbyshire does. Like Nottingham it was built by King Henry II and stands on the edge of a precipitous cliff.

curtain walls – encircling stone defences. It has an early-twelfth-century keep with enormously thick walls similar to the plain square tower at the heart of Nottingham Castle. The keep still suggests the severity of life in a medieval fortress. There is now no great hall at Peveril, but one at Winchester still survives, built within a lifetime of the hall at Nottingham. Although the windows have been replaced, the scars of the vast original window openings (originally unglazed) can still be seen. The great pillars supporting the roof and creating two aisles are probably similar to what was built at Nottingham.

Nottingham Castle was thrown violently into the national spotlight in the reign of Richard I. Richard the Lionheart is perhaps everyone's idea of a perfect medieval king. He is remembered as a brave knight, a crusader, a brilliant soldier, a diplomat, a devout Christian and a fair ruler. Even in his lifetime he was a legend, and has since become a royal hero, so much so that his true story has blended with the fictional life of Robin Hood, to create one of the most romantic chapters in English history. Yet despite this, and despite the fact that he was born in Oxford, he had little affection for England and did not even speak English. On his death he ordered that his brain be buried in Poitou, his heart in Normandy and his body in Anjou: England received no part of the great man's mortal remains. This was because Henry II and his son Richard were rulers not only of England, but also of lands that stretched from Hadrian's Wall to the Pyrenees. This empire centred not on England but on Anjou, in France (hence it is known as the Angevin Empire). England was important because it brought a crown, as well as huge wealth and power, but it was never the centre of Richard's concerns.

Richard's father, Henry II, was married to Eleanor of Aquitaine, who bore him four boys: Henry, Richard, Geoffrey and John. Henry II needed to keep his vast, creaking empire together with the help of his sons. As they came of age, one by one they were granted lands to support themselves. His heir Henry was granted Anjou, Maine, Touraine, Normandy and England. Richard was made Duke of Aquitaine, Geoffrey was given Brittany and eventually John was granted Ireland. Whilst this consolidated Henry's power, it also set a time bomb ticking. Henry II had come to the throne young and was only in his thirties as his empire was doled out to his sons. They in turn were forced to wait in the provinces to be given real power by their reigning father. What made this potentially difficult situation explosive was that the older boys knew that the King favoured his youngest son, John, and feared that they

Little is known about the hall at Nottingham, but it was probably
very like the great hall of Winchester Castle, built in *c.*1222–36 in
the reign of Henry III. In order for the roof to span its great width,
the hall had two aisles, seen here.

would be made to cede their powers to him as he grew older. This
led to a family squabble on a European scale, a squabble that became
even more vicious when, in 1183, Henry died of dysentery and
Richard, aged twenty-six, became heir to the English throne.

Richard was already well known. On his father's orders, he had
brought to heel the rebellious barons of Aquitaine in a series of
spectacularly successful sieges. And in 1187 he started a course of
action that would bring him worldwide fame. That November
Richard 'took the Cross', a symbolic act by which he took a
piece of fabric in the shape of a cross and had it stitched to his
over-garment as a symbol that he was to crusade against the infidel
in the Holy Land. Richard's decision was a reaction to the dis-
turbing news that the Saracens, under their leader Saladin, had

captured the Holy City of Jerusalem. Richard's determination to crusade against him led to a denouement in the Angevin family crisis that saw open warfare break out between the brothers and their father. In the midst of this, in 1189, Henry II died a broken and disappointed man, leaving Richard king of England.

Richard was crowned in Westminster Abbey on 3 September amidst lavish ceremonial and the disconcerting knowledge that immediately afterwards he would be leaving England for at least a year. While there was popular enthusiasm for the idea of a crusade, the risks of an absentee King were only too obvious to the ruling classes. Not only would his absence cause squabbling and rivalry amongst the great barons, but it would almost certainly ignite another Angevin family row. Given this, Richard was careful to make arrangements to secure his throne while he was away. Before he left he decided to set his younger brother up with valuable gifts of land, believing that the great wealth these would bring him would keep John in check. Richard granted his brother Nottinghamshire, Derbyshire, Cornwall, Devon, Dorset and Somerset – almost a third of the kingdom, virtually an independent principality in itself, and the largest area of land held by one subject since the Conquest. Although at first sight this seems like an extraordinarily lavish gift, it was in fact a gilded insult. These lands were the estates that belonged to the great castles of the realm, but although John got the land, Richard withheld the castles, which he kept in his own hands. So John got the wealth but not the power. He now had all the great lands that surrounded Nottingham Castle, even the fine hunting lodges nearby like Clipstone, but not the Castle itself. As Richard embarked for France he left England in the hands of his most loyal minister, William Longchamp, Bishop of Ely. In Normandy he summoned his two brothers, John and Geoffrey, and made them swear that they would not enter England for three years. If John had ambitions to usurp his brother while he was away, it was going to be very difficult.

In July 1190, after raising money and troops on the Continent, Richard set off on crusade from Vézelay in central France. The size of his army was probably only a few thousand, as many as he could

realistically support over the vast distance that he had to travel.
Working to a carefully predetermined plan, the army was to move
via Sicily to take Cyprus as a supply base and then sail to the
besieged town of Acre, the largest and most important port in the
Kingdom of Jerusalem. After lifting the siege there Richard's target
would be Jerusalem itself.

After successfully taking Cyprus, Richard left for the Holy Land,
arriving at Acre on 8 June. He was welcomed with glee by the
international crusading force that had been besieging the city for
eighteen months. Acre was built on a short promontory protruding
into the Mediterranean, forming a natural harbour. Crusading ships
blockaded the coast, while on land the crusader army encircled the
city. Richard's experience, equipment and men tipped the balance
and Acre fell. His army moved off down the coast, winning the
glorious battle of Arsuf on the way. In fact Richard reached the
very gates of Jerusalem, only to turn away when he realized that to
take it would be difficult and to hold it impossible. To this huge
disappointment was added some incredibly bad news. In April 1192
Richard learned that his greatest fears had been realized: all was not
well in England. John, Longchamp and the barons were fighting
each other, and his empire was imperilled. The King had no choice
but to pack his bags and return home. Richard's long return trip
ended in disaster: he was shipwrecked and fell into the hands of
Duke Leopold of Austria, who imprisoned him in Castle Durnstein,
not far from Vienna. Richard, the great hero of the crusades,
supposedly under the protection of the Church, had suddenly
become the most valuable, and the most hopeless, pawn in Europe.

As Richard left for his crusade a sense of dark foreboding spread
across England. Those who knew Prince John realized that he was
not likely to be placated by his new responsibilities, and certainly
not constrained by orders to stay in France (which in any case were
countermanded by Richard soon after). At the very least he would
probably be consumed by a determination to take the castles that
he had not received with his lands; at worst he might make a bid
for the throne. Failure and bad luck had dogged John for most of
his life. He had lived in the daunting shadow of his glamorous

brother Richard and saw his own military exploits flop beside his brother's successes. Although none of the epithets he was given stuck like his brother's 'Lionheart', he had no shortage of them. He was dubbed 'Lackland', 'Softsword' and 'Coeur de Poupée' or 'Doll's Heart'. But John was no fool – he was a charming and capable politician and found it easy to win support amongst the powerful Angevin barons. In this he was unwittingly helped by Richard's chancellor and regent William Longchamp, who was acting in an overbearing and domineering way towards the barons.

The flashpoint was Longchamp's ill-treatment of one of Richard's most powerful barons, Gerard de Camville, who was deprived of his offices and had his castle at Lincoln besieged by the Chancellor. John used this as an excuse to persuade the constables of nearby Tickhill and Nottingham to hand over their castles to him. Although after the Lincoln siege the castles were taken back from John and the constables punished, they were firmly back in his control when news of his brother's capture arrived. By the time the Emperor Henry VI finally secured Richard's release in February 1194, John had already entered into a treaty with the King of France and proclaimed himself King of England. As news of Richard's release spread across Europe with all the speed the twelfth century could muster, John was faced with a dilemma: should he hold out against his brother or capitulate? He decided to fight. Letters were sent out to the castles he had seized, with orders to hold out against Richard. More by luck than design, John's orders fell into the hands of Richard's royal council, and even before Richard had landed the great lords and bishops loyal to him were besieging John's illegally-held fortresses. While the Bishop of Durham, at the head of a large army, besieged Tickhill Castle and the Archbishop of Canterbury laid siege to Marlborough, Nottingham stood out as the greatest challenge. It was the strongest castle in John's hands, and whoever held it controlled the Midlands and a major route north. Three earls – Huntingdon, Chester and Ferrers – were sent to deal with Nottingham, each with local knowledge and a local power base for raising troops.

Even if temperamentally Richard had not loved a fight, even if he had not been addicted to the notion of siege warfare, he would have had no choice but to march straight to the Midlands to reclaim his castles. This was a direct challenge to his authority and to the Crown itself – and, it must be remembered, a Crown that ruled over much of France as well as England. The fate of the Angevin Empire literally hung in the balance. As King Richard, bristling with indignation and spoiling for a fight, marched north with his army, William de Wenneval and Roger de Muntbegun, John's two constables in Nottingham Castle, were already under siege. They were probably well prepared and had stocked the castle with provisions and garrisoned it with a full fighting force. They would have recruited surgeons to tend to the injured, masons to repair damaged defences, cooks to feed the garrison, and blacksmiths and fletchers to keep the soldiers equipped. John was in France, and so communication with their overlord would have been very difficult; thus this force, although well prepared, must have felt very isolated.

By the time Richard reached the Midlands, nearby Tickhill Castle had capitulated to the Bishop of Durham, the defenders having been persuaded that Richard's return was genuine and that without surrender they would be executed as traitors. The situation at Nottingham was very different: the defenders had made no attempt to communicate with their besiegers, and they refused to believe Richard had returned, or perhaps thought the news a trick. On 25 March Richard Coeur de Lion himself stood outside the gates of his own castle waiting to wreak revenge. The King was attended by a substantial army with all the equipment he needed to conduct a full and prolonged siege. It is inconceivable that the defenders knew that Richard was at the head of this force. Not only was he their king, but he was the most formidable and brutal soldier in Europe. He had returned from fighting a war with the latest technology against the most powerful and modern castles in the world. Such was his reputation that when another of John's rebel commanders, the constable of Mont St Michel, heard that Richard had returned, he allegedly dropped dead from fright.

Richard immediately set up camp in a house near the castle, mainly so that he could be seen, but partly to allow him to direct the siege personally. His first target was to capture the outer ward. The castle's outer defences were still almost certainly earthworks topped with timber ramparts, but they were nonetheless strong, and certainly well guarded by the garrison. Impetuously Richard, impatient to make progress, personally led a direct attack on the outer gatehouse, raining arrows down on the rebels before taking it by storm. At the head of his troops he fought his way through the outer ward, repelling a sortie from the castle and capturing the barbican (outer defence) in front of the middle ward gatehouse. After only a day's fighting the outer ward was the King's. His prisoners were hanged from a gallows in full sight of the castle walls as a warning of what was to come. But Richard was now faced with a much greater challenge: the middle and inner wards built in stone only twenty years earlier, incorporating all the latest defensive features. Heavily fortified towers allowing defenders to protect the flank of the curtain walls from besiegers encircled the castle. From wall-walks on the battlements archers could look down on their opponents, commanding the area below. There was a great gate-house, probably featuring the latest defensive devices, including a drawbridge and portcullis. In short the King was faced with one of England's most impregnable fortresses.

Richard had a worldwide reputation in siege warfare. He knew better than anyone that to breach a castle's defences was an extremely difficult, lengthy and expensive process. To succeed, the right equipment had to be transported and deployed, and skilled operatives had to be on hand. Above all, patience was required – success was rarely instant. Before the invention of artillery the most important weapon in a siege was a rock-throwing machine known as a mangonel (see Plate 8). A long wooden beam with a sling attached to the end was pulled down against the tension of twisted ropes and then released to fling a rock through the air. The repeated stress on the ropes gradually lessened the tension and reduced the range of the mangonel over time. This meant that it had to be drawn ever closer to its target and, of course, to the unrelenting onslaught of arrows and missiles from the castle. Richard was particularly adept at the positioning and use of the mangonel.

Famously at the siege of Acre he rejected the Palestinian limestone boulders that other crusader armies had used, having brought with him instead massive lumps of iron-like Sicilian granite. These did not break up on impact like the soft limestone but smashed their way though the city defences. The besieged often had catapults of their own, and one medieval account describes the rocks from besieged and besieger dramatically colliding and smashing in mid-air. A particularly gruesome method of lowering morale and spreading disease among the besieged was to substitute the severed heads and other body parts of their fallen comrades for rocks and lob them over the castle walls.

Another siege technique that Richard had perfected in Palestine was the use of fire. This was an effective mode of attack since stone castles were constructed with wooden beams and planks for doors, roofs and floors. Burning arrows and torches could be shot over the defences to cause mayhem inside. This was literally a hit-and-miss affair because seasoned oak is difficult to ignite and exposed timbers were often covered with lead or water-soaked animal skins to make them less vulnerable. Likewise gatehouses were almost always equipped with so-called murder holes that would allow water to be poured on bonfires lit against timber castle gates. Yet a castle like Nottingham often had thatched roofs in the inner ward, a tempting target to attackers. A more successful method of destruction was the use of the much-feared Greek fire. This highly combustible material was a mixture of sulphur, petroleum, saltpetre and quicklime, and it ignited on impact. It got its name from the Byzantine Greeks who used it in naval warfare. Greek fire was particularly devastating because it could not be extinguished by water. Well-equipped castles would set aside barrels of vinegar to put out the fire, the only sure means of success.

Undermining the walls of a castle was probably the most effective method of attack. Miners were brought in to tunnel under the stone defences, temporarily supporting the foundations from beneath with vast wooden props. Special wooden covers reinforced by tin, lead or skins protected the coming and going of miners, their spoil and props (see Plate 9). Once the mine was complete the void would be filled with combustible material and ignited. As the main props burnt away, the undermined section of the wall would come crashing down. Sometimes pigs covered in burning tar would be driven into the mine to light the subterranean bonfire – much safer than sending a man inside. Mines were by far the most feared form of attack, since often the first the defenders knew of them was the smell of smoke or collapsing ramparts beneath their feet. If a mining operation was spotted from the walls the only way to impede progress was to burrow down on the inside of the castle and attack the miners underground. As most castles and fortified cities were eventually taken through the use of the mine, castle designers added massive splayed bases (batters) to corner towers and turrets to give the outer walls an extra degree of stability.

Another piece of equipment that Richard was adept at using was the siege tower. This was essentially a vast protected timber staircase, which could be rolled into position to allow the attackers direct access to the ramparts. Battering rams and bores were also used to smash through gates and walls. A battering ram was usually a tree trunk with iron bands, sometimes suspended by chains from a frame, at other times simply carried by heavily armoured men. On these occasions the murder holes in the gatehouse would be used by the defenders for pouring molten lead or scalding sand on the attackers. Sand, a seemingly innocuous weapon, could trickle down inside armour and cause terrible burns.

Whilst all these techniques were helpful, the key to success was well-trained foot soldiers. They were obviously armed with swords and daggers, but their most deadly weapon was the arrow. The infantry crossbow developed from the great wheeled 'ballistas' which fired mighty iron bolts or spears to smash through ramparts, gateways and men. The hand-held model that formed the backbone of the English army was ferociously effective. So much so that it was outlawed by the Pope in the Second Lateran Council of 1139 except against the devil-worshipping Saracens. However, this did not prevent Richard from using it widely. The longbow was more widely used in battle from the thirteenth century onwards. Unlike the crossbow, which was generally aimed at a specific target, longbows were most often used to create a rain of arrows from which there was no escape. At any one second during a battle 1,000 arrows shot by a force of 500 archers could be soaring through the sky to rain down on the enemy. They had a range of 200 to 300 metres and their arched trajectory meant that they could be shot over castle ramparts to prevent them being reinforced. Some chronicles describe the sky being black with arrows.

All these techniques Richard had at his disposal in March 1194 as he was faced with the inner walls of Nottingham. But as night fell fighting stopped and Richard's men set light to the gatehouse of the outer ward. From the inner ward the rebel constables still loyal to John would have seen the orange glow of flames from the burning outer defences. In the middle ward there would have been a scene of chaos. It is quite clear that there had been many casualties and the great hall, normally the scene of feasting, entertainment and government, would probably have been commandeered as battle HQ and field hospital. As the largest building in the castle it would have contained men eating, drinking, sleeping and screaming in agony as medieval surgery did its worst. Disease was by far the greatest killer in war, and wounds were quickly infected. It was common knowledge that unless stopped a gangrenous wound would spread through the body and result in death. Amputations were cauterized or seared by burning hot metal or molten pitch in order to stop infection; but amputation was far more frequent than successful. Anaesthetics were unknown, but being blind drunk helped. Duke Leopold of Austria, Richard's jailer, was unfortunate enough to have his horse fall on his foot in November 1194. The next day the surgeons advised that the blackened foot should be removed, but no one in his household could bear to do it, not even his son. The Duke was forced to hold the blade of an axe against his leg while his servant tried to force it through with a mallet. He didn't survive for long.

Arrow wounds were probably the most common problem. Being shot by a barbed arrow was devastating, and archers often tipped their arrowheads with beeswax to lubricate the tips and help them to penetrate the tight chain mail worn by the enemy. Surgeons would attempt to remove the arrows with what implements they had, but the chances of survival were low. The best one could hope for was the arrow to go right through: at least that way surgery could be avoided. It was a bolt from a crossbow that was eventually to kill Richard. He was shot at the insignificant siege of Châlus-Chabrol by a lone defender defying the King at twilight with a frying pan for a shield. The bolt entered his shoulder and in his attempt to pull it out Richard broke the wooden shaft, leaving a large iron barb embedded in his flesh. Working at night by dim torchlight the royal surgeon managed to extract the barb, but not without mangling the King's shoulder. Under the carefully applied bandages gangrene grew and spread, killing the King within ten days.

Despite the chaos inside Nottingham Castle on the night of 25 March the castle was far from lost. Richard may have taken the outer bailey, but he was now faced with the stone middle and inner wards. Early the next morning, on the rising land to the north of the castle, Richard's siege engines were being assembled under heavy protection from snipers on the castle walls. By the end of the day they were probably hurling boulders at the castle. At this stage it seems as if the defenders realized that they were up against no ordinary opponent.

The prolonged and costly nature of siege warfare allowed for the development of a number of conventions. It was customary for the two sides to parley (or talk) at the commencement of the siege. The Nottingham defenders had been given their chance to accept the King, but had thought it a trap. The basic convention from then on was that the besieged would be given time to receive support from their master or lord. If they had not received help by the due date then they could surrender with a degree of honour. The date could be arranged at the beginning of a siege, or well into it when the besieged were in dire straits and a truce could be called. At any point a parley could be engineered, and that is what happened on 26 March at Nottingham. Two knights were sent out of the castle by the constables to see for themselves whether the King was really there. They were brought before Richard as he sat at his dinner table and returned to the castle with the devastating news that they were holding out against the King. Wenneval and Muntbegun themselves then came out with twelve of their commanders: on seeing the King they immediately surrendered. Soon after that the whole garrison filed out of the castle and laid down their arms.

The siege was won, the crisis over, and the King secure on his throne. After a hunting trip to Sherwood Forest, Richard reclaimed his royal apartments in the castle and held a four-day council there, probably in the keep. John was forgiven, and when he became king was to rebuild the timber outer ward in stone. The siege of 1194 was certainly the most important and spectacular moment in Nottingham's history during the Middle Ages, but it was essentially a fight between princes: what happened in the 1640s was more surprising – this was a fight between the princes and the people. In January 1642 King Charles I made a botched attempt to arrest five Members of Parliament who he believed were the ringleaders of parliamentary opposition against him. In doing so he stirred up such a degree of disorder and opposition in London that on the night of 10 January he fled the capital. From that moment he had lost London, and armed conflict was almost a certainty. The King sent his French wife, Henrietta Maria, to the Continent to raise support, while he moved, with the Prince of Wales, to York, gathering loyal members of the aristocracy as he went. In everything but name the English Civil War had now begun.

The King's most pressing need was to raise an army, and he needed a base from which to do this. The choice of a base was crucial: it had to be in a royalist area, well defended, and easily reinforced from the sea with troops raised by the Queen. Warrington in Cheshire was the first choice, since it lay amidst the lands of the royalist Stanley dynasty. But Charles thought it entailed too long a voyage for the troops that he hoped the Queen would bring from the Netherlands. After some debate Nottingham was chosen – partly for its strength, partly because the Trent provided an artery to the open sea, and partly because the people round about were believed to be loyal. There may have been another reason too.

Undoubtedly Nottingham Castle was still a symbol of royal authority, and perhaps (and it is only perhaps) Charles knew that it was the place where King Richard the Lionheart had exerted his authority over rebellious subjects 450 years before. Was there a deliberate symbolism in choosing Nottingham for his stand against treasonous subjects? Would Charles Stuart's advance on Nottingham be as successful as Richard Plantagenet's?

Charles left York with 1,500 cavalry and a few troops of infantry and made for Nottingham. On his way the King made two important proclamations. The first was against the Earl of Essex, whom Parliament had appointed commander-in-chief of their forces in July. He and his fellow officers were ordered to surrender their commissions in the rebel army or be proclaimed as traitors. Then on 12 August Charles issued a proclamation charging all good and loyal subjects to meet him at Nottingham for a formal declaration of war.

By the mid seventeenth century Nottingham was a prosperous market town of about 5,000 people, still walled and dominated by the castle. Although the castle had remained the principal royal fortress in the Midlands through the sixteenth century, very little had been done to repair it or adapt it for the needs of modern artillery warfare. The simple truth was that Nottingham was a castle built to secure internal stability rather than to repel foreign invaders. Under the stable rule of the Tudors and James I, the nation's defensive efforts had been concentrated on coastal defences to prevent invasion by the Catholic powers of Europe. Nottingham Castle, under the control of its constable, was left to decline gently. It was not alone. During the later Elizabethan years and into the reign of James I all the great royal castles of England slid into gentle dereliction. The lack of a future military role, combined with Elizabeth and James's love of modern unfortified houses, ensured that castles were sidelined as royal architectural priorities. John Smythson's plan of Nottingham Castle, dated 1617, may have been the result of a royal survey to ascertain its condition. It shows a building in an advanced state of decay: the great hall had already been demolished and other buildings dismantled and unroofed. In

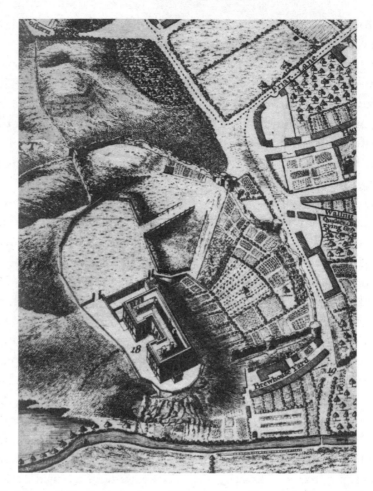

Bladder and Peat's 1744 map of Nottingham shows the Restoration ducal palace on the site of the upper bailey, but also importantly some of the masonry walls of the outer bailey still standing. In Richard the Lionheart's time these were of timber, but when his brother John came to the throne he rebuilt the outer ward in stone.

fact by 1622 James had no more use for the building and sold it to the Earl of Rutland, who began to use it as a quarry for building materials. By 1643 a report stated that the castle buildings were 'very ruinous and uninhabitable, neither affording room to lodge soldiers nor provisions'. It was to this ruined and alienated fortress that Charles I, King of England, arrived.

In the event the townsmen of Nottingham greeted him coolly and Charles decided to move on rapidly to nearby Coventry in the hope of a more enthusiastic reception. The plan was flawed because Coventry was not only pro-Parliament but was also defended by a circuit of well-maintained walls and gates. As the royalist guns began to make an impact on the fourteenth-century walls the town garrison and an advancing parliamentary force drove off the King's men. Charles reverted to his first plan and entered Nottingham unopposed, but unwelcome.

We don't know where the royal party stayed (probably not in the castle as it was too ruinous), but most of the troops would have erected tents within the castle walls. Charles probably planned to stay a few weeks after his declaration of war, since assembling a mighty royalist army would take time. Meanwhile the royalist camp stood on ceremony. Charles liked everything to be done according to ancient royal precedent, emphasizing his royal dignity and right to the throne. This gave the royal heralds a problem. It had been hundreds of years since an English king had ceremoniously declared war on his rebellious subjects and they were quite unclear what the proper etiquette was. What was clear was that the central act of the ceremony should be the unfurling of a great flag bearing the royal arms – the royal standard. At first they suggested that the standard should be unfurled from a turret window high up on the castle walls for all to see. Charles disagreed: he thought it much better to plant it on a hill to the north of the castle, later known as Standard Hill.

At any rate the event was a flop. What the King and his heralds had hoped would be a magnificent rabble-rousing spectacle, brimming with heraldry, was a damp squib. It was pouring with rain and a gale was blowing. As the King, accompanied by his cousins Prince Rupert and Prince Maurice and a small troop of cavalry, stood by in the rain, the herald attempted to read the proclamation. Charles had made several alterations to the document at the last moment and big raindrops smudged the barely dry ink, making the document almost illegible. At the end of the stumbling royal declaration the men cried 'God Save the King' and Sir Edmund

A true and exact Relation of the

manner of his Maiesties setting up of His

Standard at *Nottingham*, on Munday the
22. of August. 1642.

First, The forme of the Standard, as it is here figured, and who were present at the advancing of it

Secondly, The danger of setting up of former Standards, and the damage
which ensued thereon.

Thirdly, A relation of all the Standards that ever were set up by any King.

Fourthly, the names of those Knights who are appointed to be the Kings
Standard-bearers. With the forces that are appoynted to guard it.

Fifthly, The manner of the Kings comming first to *Coventry*.

Sixtly, The *Cavalieres* resolution and dangerous threats which they have
uttered, if the King concludes a peace without them, or hearkens unto
his great Councell the Parliament : Moreover how they have shared
and divided *London* amongst themselves already.

Nottingham.

This woodcut, part of a broadsheet describing the raising of the
royal standard at Nottingham in 1642, is the only contemporary
depiction of that fateful event.

Verney, Knight Marshall, placed the standard in a hastily excavated hole in the ground. Later that night it was prophetically blown down in the storm that still raged.

This event was typical of Charles's attitude to the Civil War. While he agonized over the correct etiquette – where to raise banners, and precisely how to word his declarations – the parliamentary forces were training men and gathering equipment. Old England was to meet new England, and the new was destined to win. Yet the King got one thing right: today a walk round Standard Hill in Nottingham reveals at least three plaques commemorating the exact spot where the royal standard so briefly fluttered. Even now, despite the scarring of Nottingham's remarkable historic skyline with ugly tower blocks, one can't help seeing King Charles's point. From any of the sites a standard held high would have been seen by the populace of Nottingham. Charles had an eye to the theatrical, one of the most important attributes of a monarch.

In the end not only was royal ceremonial ineffective, but so was the appeal for people to join the royalist army. Charles and his advisors should have known better. It was harvest time and men simply could not be spared from the fields if the population were not to starve that winter. Moreover the King had no money to buy support – even the gift, by the University of Oxford, of all their fine medieval plate, was not enough to finance a royal army. Worse still the King had lost control of the Navy and any hopes of Continental reinforcements coming up the Trent were dashed by a parliamentary naval blockade. On 13 September Charles and his small army left Nottingham for the west in the face of an advancing parliamentary army led by Essex.

Soon the castle was in parliamentarian hands under the control of Colonel John Hutchinson. He ordered a battery to be built in front of the castle gate to mount his artillery on, and presumably made enough repairs to give his garrison shelter. He also dug protective earthworks round the Trent Bridge to guard the crossing. In the castle he assembled a great arsenal of weapons and a garrison of 400 men, and from here he secured the whole of Nottinghamshire. In May 1643 Oliver Cromwell entered Nottingham and remained for almost three weeks, staying in the castle. In September the royalist Sir John Byron, the owner of nearby Newstead Abbey, and ancestor of the great poet, led a raiding party in an attempt to retake Nottingham. He quickly overwhelmed the decayed defences of the town and moved on the castle, setting up his headquarters in St Nicholas's Church. Churches were often requisitioned during military manoeuvres in the Civil War. They were large buildings with excellent observation towers, often in walled enclosures. St Nicholas's was on a hill facing the castle and not only served as a spying post but as a gun emplacement for Byron's troops. Musketeers stationed on the church tower made it almost impossible for the castle defenders to use their new gun battery.

Nottingham Castle was, after a space of 450 years, once again under siege. Hutchinson soon succeeded in manning his gun battery, reinforcing it by means of a trench from the castle which gave cover from the cavaliers positioned on the church tower. Four days of sporadic gunfire resulted, with neither side making much impression on the other. On the fifth day Hutchinson and his men were relieved by one Captain White and his troop of horse, who drove Byron off after a skirmish. A number of royalists were killed and a larger number captured and frog-marched to the castle. There some were locked in the castle chapel and others, less fortunate, were thrown into a dungeon known as the Lion's Den. The wounded parliamentarians were brought to the castle in too great a number for the garrison surgeon to cope. Lucy Hutchinson, the wife of the Governor, had them brought to her rooms in the upper ward. Lucy was a remarkable woman, whose mother had assisted Sir Walter Raleigh in his chemical experiments when he was imprisoned in the Tower of London. From her mother she had learnt how to make poultices and balsams – a skill that was to stand her in good stead as the wife of one of Parliament's colonels. After dressing the wounds of the parliamentarians she, together with the wives of the parliamentarian officers, prepared a great victory feast at the castle. Local gentlemen loyal to Parliament as well as the victorious officers sat down in the old royal apartments in the upper ward to celebrate the castle's liberation. But the royal rooms were

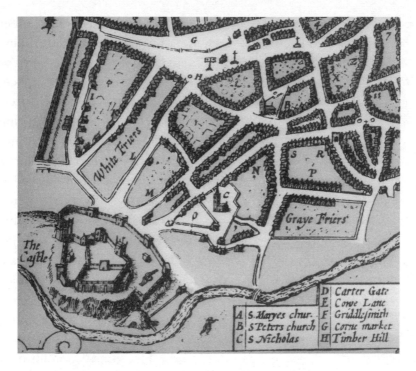

The map legend reads:

A	S. Mayes chur.	D	Carter Gate
B	S Peters church	E	Cowe Lane
C	S Nicholas	F	Griddlesmith
		G	Corne market
		H	Timber Hill

John Speed's map of 1614 taken from *Theatre of the Empire of Great Britain* shows the castle with the middle ward divided into two by a battlemented wall. The cliffs and the River Leen are clearly shown. St Nicholas's Church, demolished by Parliamentarian troops in late 1643, is marked *C*.

far bigger and the feast more plentiful than there were guests to enjoy them and so Hutchinson sent for some of the more fashionable prisoners to join them. This, combined with the fact that Lucy had also tended the injuries of three badly wounded cavaliers, caused an outburst from his fellow officers. One Captain Palmer stormed out of the banquet hurling abuse at the Governor. Why should he, one of the godly, share his meat with malignants? Why should a Levite sit down with a Samaritan? The compassion of the Hutchinsons was a rare moment of humanity in the otherwise brutal history of Nottingham Castle.

As a result of this short but bloody siege, Hutchinson ordered that St Nicholas's Church be demolished and that houses near the castle be cleared to remove cover for future attackers. The townspeople had to acquiesce to their church being dismantled, but refused to let the Governor flatten their houses. Hutchinson was proved right in July 1644 when another royalist raiding party, this time from the King's stronghold at Newark, captured the town after a dawn raid but were soon driven off by parliamentary fire from the castle ramparts.

It seems extraordinary, given the efficiency of the 1194 siege, that four and a half centuries later the fight for Nottingham was so chaotic and ineffectual. The reality was that the men who fought the Civil War and besieged dilapidated castles like Nottingham were amateurs, unschooled in the art of siege warfare. It wasn't the thickness of the medieval walls that kept Colonel Hutchinson safe from the royalist attackers: it was their incompetence. The great curtain walls of Nottingham would have quickly collapsed if they had been subjected to well-aimed intensive fire.

Parliament's experiences at castles like Pontefract, Newark and Nottingham confirmed that these crumbling fortresses could be a significant irritant, and it was decided to demolish any of them that might prove a threat again. This was a controversial policy but one that became a matter of necessity once Parliament realized that it could not afford to garrison every old castle in England against possible seizure by royalist troops. There were two options. Some castles were slighted – that is to say that their outer defences were breached and partially demolished while their inner parts were left intact. This rendered them useless defensively but saved the enormous cost of complete demolition. Today castles like Corfe in Devon and Kenilworth in Warwickshire are examples of castles slighted by Parliament and now visited by millions, who admire their romantic silhouettes. The alternative was complete demolition. This was the fate of the truly important strategic castles like Pontefract, Banbury and Nottingham. In May 1651 the Council of State ordered Nottingham Castle to be razed to the ground.

By 1651 Hutchinson had been replaced by Major Poulton, and so it was he who received orders to demolish the castle within two weeks. This was an absurdly short length of time, and in the end it took from July to November. Poulton was allowed to keep the materials from the demolition as long as he sent all military equipment, by river, to London. He did a very thorough job, removing from the site all the residential buildings and most of the defences. The stone he sold, making a handsome profit. Bladder and Peat's map of 1744 (above) suggests that he may have left some of the walls of the outer ward to enclose the former castle site, which he bought for himself.

Nottingham Castle, built as a symbol of Norman oppression, was twice the scene of a violent attempt by the English Crown to exert its authority over rebellious subjects. This is certainly one of the reasons why Parliament ordered it to be so thoroughly destroyed. It may also be the reason why it became associated with Robin Hood. Robin Hood no more existed than Father Christmas. He was already a legendary figure by the late fourteenth century, but not associated with Sherwood Forest or Nottingham Castle. In early ballads he came from Yorkshire, although some of his adventures took place in and around Nottingham. Yet most versions of the story have the Sheriff of Nottingham as his chief adversary, and by the fifteenth century Robin Hood was closely associated with Nottingham Castle. By 1485 there was even a road called Robinhode Closse in Nottingham town. Robin Hood was, in fact, probably a composite of many outlaws and criminals who stood in people's minds for a resistance to royal officials. He was a popular hero, a symbol of liberty. That Robin Hood's principal adversary resided at the ultimate symbol of royal authority is no surprise.

After the Civil War William Cavendish, the first Duke of Newcastle, bought the site of the castle and on it he built a remarkable Italianate palace. This new building dominated Nottingham and its surroundings no less than the medieval castle before it. On 10 October 1831 a furious mob of Nottingham townsmen stormed the ducal palace and set it alight (see Plate 10). The fabulous structure and its glittering interiors were completely gutted. The mob had been incensed by the rejection in the House of Lords, enthusiastically supported by the Duke of Newcastle, of a Parliamentary Reform Bill to extend the franchise and end electoral abuses. Seven hundred and fifty years after its foundation and 180 years after its demolition Nottingham Castle was still a symbol of oppression and attacking it was still a blow for liberty. Nottingham Castle was architecture as tyranny – the secret of its success but also the seeds of its fall.

Millbank Penitentiary

The Reformation of the Criminal Mind

Millbank Penitentiary was Britain's first national prison, and the largest and most ambitious, built to reform rather than merely incarcerate criminals. When it was completed in 1822 it was the largest prison in Europe, covering sixteen acres, designed to house 1,000 prisoners and built at a cost of £458,000. Its promoters saw it as a model for the world, the finest and most modern institution for the reformation of the criminal mind. Yet only twenty-seven years later a parliamentary committee declared it an 'entire failure'. How could a building devised by the best minds of the day, costing more than any other public building up to that time, be such a complete flop? And how did this failed experiment ultimately lead to the penal system of today?

The idea of Millbank Penitentiary grew out of eighteenth-century philanthropy, humanism, religion and philosophy. From the beginning of the eighteenth century critics began to comment on the miserable conditions found in prisons throughout the country. Prisoners were thrown together regardless of their sex, age or crime. Once imprisoned they were left to their own devices and passed the time boozing, gambling and whoring. The gaolers were like brutal innkeepers, extorting fees for food, drink and minor comforts and conveniences. The authorities showed little interest in religion and even less concern about general behaviour unless, of course, it threatened the security of the prison.

When, in 1776, William Smith wrote a report on the prisons of London, he opened his description as follows:

> Few, accustomed to any degree of cleanliness, could bear the stench of such places, or stand the shock of such misery. Vagrants and

disorderly women of the very lowest and most wretched class of human beings, almost naked, with only a few filthy rags almost alive and in motion with vermin, their bodies rotting with the bad distemper, and covered with itch, scorbutic and venereal ulcers . . . there thirty, and sometimes near forty of these unhappy wretches are crouded or crammed together in one ward, where in the dark they bruise and beat one another in a most shocking manner.

. . . [The warders are] obliged to drink a glass of spirits to keep them from fainting, for the putrid steam or miasma is enough to knock them down. They are frequently seized with such violent reaching, that nothing will lie upon their stomachs . . . When the turnkeys are so affected by only opening doors, what must the miserable wretches, confined the whole night in such putrid hot-beds of disease suffer?

Yet mid-eighteenth-century philanthropic concern about these terrible conditions made little impact on the prison system, partly because most people believed that the awful conditions of prison served as a deterrent to the would-be law-breaker. The man who was eventually to break the impasse and make of prison reform a pressing national concern was John Howard. Born in 1726, he was originally destined for the grocery business but with his father's death he inherited a considerable fortune which he used to fund a number of philanthropic schemes in local housing, schooling and employment. In 1773, in recognition of his efforts, he was elected high sheriff of Bedfordshire. Howard took this role seriously and among his duties was the management of the county gaol. Far from letting things run themselves as they had for generations, Howard took an active interest in the prison and was appalled to find people incarcerated after their sentence was up simply because they could not afford a discharge fee. To him it was obvious that the only way to stop the exploitation of prisoners was to provide gaolers with a salary independent of the tolls they squeezed from their wards and so he asked the Bedfordshire magistrates to organize this. Perhaps not surprisingly they were reluctant unless some precedent could be found. Howard responded by trying to find one. In his unsuccessful

One of William Hogarth's series of prints *The Rake's Progress*, chronicling the decline and fall of a rich young man. This scene shows him in an eighteenth-century debtor's prison. It was this sort of prison that reformers like Howard were trying to close.

research he discovered that most prisons were filthy, stinking, miserable places for prisoners and gaolers alike, filled with injustice and depravity. He found a prison in Exeter without water or sewerage. In Ely gaol, under the management of the bishop, prisoners were fastened to the floor by chains and spiked collars, their legs bound by heavy iron bars unless they could pay for them to be removed. Nearly half the local prisons in England were in the hands of private owners, who made a healthy income from them: Richard Ackerman, gaoler of the principal London prison of Newgate for thirty-eight years, left the enormous sum of £20,000 when he died in 1792.

In many gaols prisoners not only had to pay for the 'easement of irons' and freedom from torture but also the basics of survival. In some gaols it was common to feed the inmates from scraps thrown by passers-by through the door or at a window box that the prisoners took turns to sit by. Prisoners in the debtors' ward in Exeter begged by lowering a shoe on the end of a string from a window. Locals even called the prison 'the shoe'. The lack of segregation led to prisons becoming breeding grounds for venereal diseases, and many inmates died or went mad from syphilis. Pregnancy and birth were common too, with mothers and children frequently dying in filthy conditions. To keep prisoners confined and to avoid window tax, many prisons had no windows at all, so that the foetid stench was almost unbearable. Typhus was common: in fact Howard claimed that 'gaol fever' killed more prisoners than the noose in 1773–4.

Within a year of taking office as sheriff, Howard gave evidence to the House of Commons in support of legislation for salaried gaolers paid for by local rates, an end to discharge fees, and new standards of health and hygiene within prisons. By his efforts the Discharged Prisoners Act and the Health of the Prisoners Act were passed in 1774. Although the latter attempted to drastically reform the condition of local prisons, it was difficult to implement and frequently ignored at a local level. It demanded that prisons should be ventilated, supplied with baths, cleaned regularly, and white-washed on a yearly basis. The sick were to be housed in separate rooms and a surgeon or apothecary was to be appointed. Furthermore, lest anyone forget, the Act itself was to be displayed conspicuously in the prison. Howard himself paid for the two Acts to be sent to every prison in the country, although he later discovered that the regulations had been closely followed in only fifteen of the 130 gaols that he inspected.

Not satisfied that everything possible was being done to reform the penal system, Howard headed off on a series of international missions to see what happened abroad. His seven tours took him to places as far afield as Malta, Moscow, Lisbon and Constantinople. On these trips Howard began to contrast the disorder he had found in England with the more enlightened approach of the most modern European institutions. He was particularly impressed by the Rasp

Houses in Amsterdam and the Maison de Force in Ghent. At the Maison de Force Howard saw, for the first time, a prison design that gave prisoners, as opposed to lunatics, cellular accommodation.

Howard published two books that were enormously influential: in 1777 *The State of English Prisons* and in 1789 *An Account of the Principal Lazarettos in Europe*. His first book set down his ideas for prison reform. Prisons, he believed, should be built near a river or stream, in a place that afforded good ventilation. Sober, well-educated and salaried gaolers should live in and be constantly on call. In a section entitled 'Plan for a County Gaol' Howard proposed a prison divided into a series of separate rectangular sections which segregated felons from debtors, men from women and children from adults, and provided each with their own yard for exercise and air. In the winter they could use a ground–floor arcade for exercise, which allowed the maximum movement of air. Above this were two floors of individual cells. Baths were to be provided for hygiene, ovens built to sterilize clothes, clean shirts distributed twice a week, and sewers were not to be placed beneath the building but beneath the courtyards. Finally he advised that prisoners' behaviour should be controlled, and they should be prevented from gambling, drinking, fighting and swearing. The most striking departure in Howard's scheme was his emphasis on the use of individual cells. In some early prisons there had been cells to isolate some prisoners, especially the condemned, but Howard's prisons were to be entirely composed of them.★

The outbreak of war in America in 1775 was a turning point in the history of prisons in England. Up to this date miscreants had been transported to Maryland and Virginia as an alternative to domestic imprisonment. Up to 1,000 criminals a year crossed the Atlantic under these arrangements. But war put a stop to this practice and something was needed to deal with the vast numbers of felons who were now crowding local gaols. Within a year an

★ Howard finally fell victim to the typhus that he had successfully resisted in the hundreds of prisons he had visited on 20 January 1790 in Kherson, just north of the Crimea. By the time of his death he was a national hero, and his commemorative statue was the first to be allowed in St Paul's Cathedral.

Act of Parliament came up with a temporary solution: prisoners would be divided between houses of correction and hulks anchored on the Thames. The hulks were former Royal Navy vessels, decommissioned and converted into prisons. They were a step backwards in prison reform: dirty, overcrowded, cold and disease-ridden. There was no segregation, no individual cells, no welfare provision. Escapes were frequent, and in the first twenty months of operation 150 out of 600 convicts died. By 1778, with the prison population exploding and prisoners dying in their hundreds, the Government was shamed into coming up with a more permanent solution to the problem. An idea to create nineteen labour camps failed, but a scheme to build national penitentiaries was enacted by Parliament in 1779: it was known as the Penitentiary Act.

Penitentiaries were to be an entirely new type of prison, heavily influenced by the ideas of Howard and his reforming colleagues. In them prisoners were to be reformed, according to the Act, through work of 'the hardest and most servile Kind, in which Drudgery is chiefly required . . . such as treading in a wheel for turning a Mill or other Machine or Engine, sawing Stone, polishing Marble, beating Hemp, rasping Logwood, chopping Rags, making Cordage'. As an incentive prisoners were allowed to keep a tiny part of the profits of their labours, which they could send to their families. When not being ground down by the monotonous toils of hard labour, they would be subjected to religious instruction or to solitary confinement, where they could ponder the wickedness of their crimes and the message of Christ at leisure. A committee was formed to put the plan into practice and John Howard was among the three supervisors chosen. However, they were plagued by rows over where to build the first of these new prisons, and after an abortive attempt to construct it in Battersea, south London, nothing was achieved: it was, in fact, to be more than thirty years before a national penitentiary was actually realized at Millbank.

A significant reason for the failure of this initiative was the revival of the alternative and much cheaper solution of transportation. From the moment the American colonies ceased to be a destination, alternatives were being sought. One suggestion was to trade English

A nineteenth-century engraving showing two prison hulks moored off Woolwich. Conditions aboard these floating prisons were even worse than in many unreformed county gaols.

criminals for prisoners captured by Muslim pirates on the coast of North Africa. Others suggested that Gambia, Tristan da Cunha, the Cape, Madagascar and Algiers might be suitable locations for new penal colonies. Finally it was decided to send them to south-eastern Australia, recently mapped and claimed for Britain by Captain Cook: the first cargo of convicts arrived at Sydney Cove in 1788. This quick and easy solution for dealing with prisoners was preferable to the expense of constructing, running and maintaining a new penitentiary.

Yet the Penitentiary Act of 1779 had a profound impact on gaols throughout the country. Further local acts concerning gaols followed and from 1780 to 1815 the great majority of local prisons were either largely rebuilt or redesigned following the principles of separation, hard work, religion and reformation. Two of the most influential and important were Gloucester Penitentiary and Southwell House of Correction. Gloucester was designed for prisoners who had been sentenced to transportation but who were considered to be candidates for reform while they were waiting. Inmates spent their time in solitary cells, only mixing with their fellows at chapel or while washing. The idea was to force on the minds of convicts the idea of living a virtuous life after they were released. Southwell was for a different type of felon. The governor of the prison claimed that they took a man 'filthy, diseased, drunken, idle and profane; and that man in a short time becomes clean, sober, healthy, diligent and to all appearances a good moral man'. The system was based on what they called 'rewarded labour', whereby the profits of the prisoner's work were split between the county, the gaoler and the prisoner. This gave the prisoner an incentive to behave and to work. Unlike Gloucester, where they were in solitary confinement, at Southwell prisoners were allowed to mix with other inmates unless they misbehaved.

The experiences in running these two reform prisons fed into the reports of two Parliamentary select committees in 1811 and 1812. These recommended the construction of a new national penitentiary based on 'the reformation and improvement of the mind, and operating by seclusion, employment and religious instruction'. The site for this new prison was to be Millbank, on the north bank of the River Thames about half a mile upstream of the Houses of Parliament. The Millbank Penitentiary was started in a spirit of enormous optimism. It was to be a machine for mending evil minds, a building that through the perfection of its design and the rigour of its internal regime was to set criminals on a path to an upright and godly life.

From Roman times, Millbank had been a boggy, marshy area of little value, and from the sixteenth century it had been used for punishing petty criminals caught in Westminster, or isolating plague victims to prevent them from spreading their deadly disease. It had been the site of an abortive attempt to build a reform prison before, but this time the weight of central government was behind the proposal. Although Millbank was a marshy bog, it was close to the Thames and therefore close to a reliable water supply and drainage. The river made the transport of building materials, supplies and prisoners very easy. It was away from polite society and had the great advantage of being within easy reach of Westminster, which meant that its day-to-day management could be under the constant surveillance of Parliament.

The design of this new building was to be crucial. Prison reformers had been obsessed with prison planning, and from the late 1770s had advocated the 'panopticon' design, the underlying principle of which was the ability of the warders to see all parts of the prison from a central vantage point. Various new types of prison, some based on the panopticon idea, but others on less idealistic principles, had been built in England since the passing of the Penitentiary Act. Yet the building at Millbank was to be the largest and most ambitious, and getting the plan right was the key to the venture's success. An architectural competition was launched and the judges considered forty-three entries. In the end the prize of £200 was awarded to W. Williams of Golden Square. Williams taught drawing at the Royal Military College at Sandhurst and was not an architect; his prison design was based on fashionable reform prisons of the day, but was a far more ambitious building. It was like a great six-petalled geometrical flower: at its heart was a circular chapel surrounded by a hexagon of administrative and service buildings. From each side of the hexagon sprang a pentagonal 'petal' of cells surrounding exercise courtyards. It was an extraordinary design: nothing like it had ever been proposed before. Its very scale, ambition and novelty meant that an amateur such as Williams could never have supervised its construction, and so it was decided to hand the task of building it to an established architect who had experience of designing prisons – Thomas Hardwick. Hardwick modified the design and wrote a specification for the new prison, calculating that it would cost £239,725 to build, with an extra £42,690 for the foundations. Work started and it immediately became clear that the boggy ground was going to be problematic. Hardwick had decided to build his walls on a substructure of wooden planks, piles and 2-feet-deep rubble footings but these proved unstable and the advice of a committee of experts was sought. But before their report on the problem was issued, Hardwick realized that he had bitten off more than he could chew. The building was enormous and supervising its complicated construction was absorbing all his time. Moreover the fee agreed for his work was only 2 per cent of the construction cost and Hardwick thought this far from adequate for a job so large. He resigned just in time, for the completed outer perimeter walls and the massive rusticated gatehouse both started to crack and subside in the summer of 1813. With Hardwick out of the firing line a new architect was appointed. He was the runner-up in the original competition, a little known architect by the name of John Harvey. He was a bad choice. He had been sacked in 1806 for the incompetent administration of Government contracts and may have seen the Millbank project as a way of winning back his reputation with the Office of Works. He certainly did not take it on for money: 2 per cent had already been proved too small a fee to attract a really top architect. For the next three years this inadequate man struggled with the problems of the massive penitentiary. Various types of foundation were proposed and tried: in the end much of the new work was built on only three layers of brick set in a very strong cement. By May 1816 a third of the prison was completed. It had already cost £128,304 and a further £230,000 was needed, nevertheless the following month the first thirty-six prisoners moved in – all women transferred from Newgate Prison in the City of London. Their first months seem to have been uneventful, but one morning in September the warders found that they could not open the cell doors. When the prison governor arrived to investigate he found the prisoners in a state of terror: one had had a fit, she was so frightened. Large cracks and fissures had appeared in the walls and turrets and the governor had to persuade the inmates that they were not about to be buried beneath hundreds of tons of collapsed masonry. After an inquiry it was concluded that the subsidence was caused by the river, which was let into the poorly built prison drains to clean them and leaked out, washing away the foundations.

Harvey left the job in disgrace, his career in ruins. This time the Government took a grip on the project. They increased the remuneration for the architect to the normal 5 per cent and employed a well-known name, Sir Robert Smirke. Smirke was

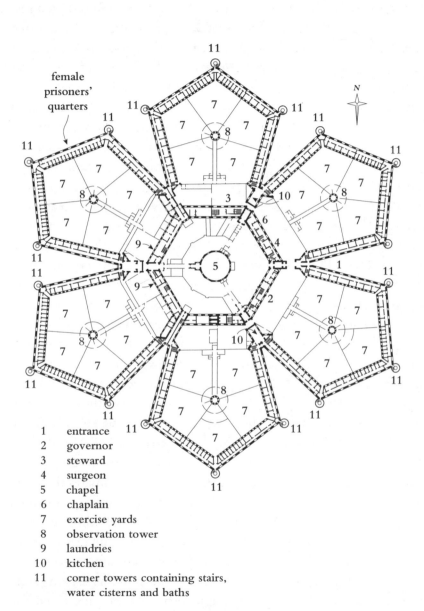

female
prisoners'
quarters

N

1   entrance
2   governor
3   steward
4   surgeon
5   chapel
6   chaplain
7   exercise yards
8   observation tower
9   laundries
10   kitchen
11   corner towers containing stairs,
     water cisterns and baths

Millbank Penitentiary as completed.

one of the most successful architects of the early nineteenth century. Apart from his undoubted architectural and engineering skills, this was due to patronage by the Tory political establishment. In 1814, at the age of thirty-three, he had become one of the three architects attached to the Office of Works, the official Government architects' department. In this role he was later responsible for designing and building such important structures as the British Museum. Smirke would never be known as a brilliant designer, but he was excellent at handling the business side of construction and was adept at solving difficult constructional conundrums. In fact he was renowned as a troubleshooter, taking on contracts and buildings that others had failed at. The crisis at Millbank was thus made for him.

Smirke rapidly identified the problem. The sewers were indeed partly to blame. They had not been built properly and water leached out of them, waterlogging the ground beneath the flimsy foundations. He quickly got to work. The building contractors were sacked, the drains were rebuilt, the towers and walls underpinned, and a new type of foundation invented for the rest of the prison. This was a concrete raft, a technique familiar to us today, but an entirely novel solution then. The raft, in places as much as 18 feet deep, spread the weight of the walls so as to give them stability. The concrete was poured so quickly and was so deep that at its core it never fully set. When recent building work at the Tate Gallery disturbed the raft, it was found that some of the cement was still wet: it only set on exposure to the air 190 years after it was laid.

All this was expensive. Hardwick had thought he could build the new prison for £259,000. Harvey's estimate had raised the cost to £350,000, but when Smirke took responsibility for the failing project the anticipated budget was £380,000. In all, the completed building cost an enormous £450,310, making it one of the most expensive public buildings ever. (As we shall see, even that was not the end of the story: Millbank prison continued to eat up public money for the rest of its existence.)

The prison, when completed in 1821, covered sixteen acres, the buildings themselves taking up about seven acres: the corridors

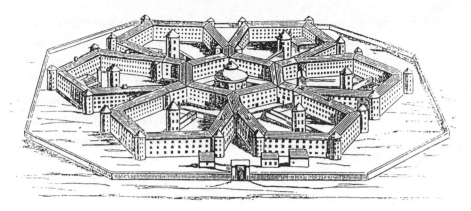

Nineteenth-century engraving of the original architect's model for Millbank Penitentiary.

alone were more than three miles in length. It was originally designed to take 800 prisoners, but during construction the plans were altered and its capacity extended to 1,000. It was an enormous, labyrinthine structure, built in three storeys with six interconnected pentagons. The whole complex was enclosed by an octagonal wall and a deep water-filled moat. When it was completed it was described as a 'gigantic puzzle' and 'one of the most successful realizations, on a large scale, of the ugly in architecture, being a combination of the mad-house with the fortress style'. A deputy governor later described the architecture as 'one of the last specimens of an age . . . when the safe custody of criminals could only be compassed by granite blocks and ponderous bolts and bars. Such notions were a legacy of medievalism, bequeathed by ruthless chieftains'. He was right: it was a grim fortress, not dissimilar to those built to repel Napoleon's navy on the south coast. This prison fortress was built largely of sandstone from the Duke of Devonshire's quarries in Derbyshire, but it also contained 10 million bricks, 2,000 iron doors and millions of tons of concrete. Gas and water were conveyed by miles of lead pipe; floors were flagged with tens of thousands of flagstones. Its construction was aided by the use of both cast- and wrought-iron girders – an extensive and early use of the technology.

It was entered through a massive rusticated gatehouse facing the

River Thames (see Plate 11). Prisoners, warders and visitors alike came in this way, their names being carefully recorded in a ledger to keep track of the number of people inside. From here a newly admitted prisoner would be taken to the governor's rooms, which occupied one side of the inner hexagon. At their heart was the governor's office, a large room divided by a rope on one side of which was his desk. New prisoners, and those accused of misconduct, would be brought to the rope for interrogation. Behind the governor's desk, hanging on the wall, was a heavy curtain, and beneath this was a large-scale plan of the whole prison at all its levels. It remained covered while prisoners were in the room to prevent them understanding the maze into which they were being welcomed.

On leaving the governor's office a new inmate would be stripped naked and taken to one of the prison bathhouses. These were situated in the three circular towers at the outer points of each pentagon. On the top of each tower was a water tank filled by a pump from the river. In each circular bathroom below there were four baths, in one of which the new prisoner would be scrubbed and disinfected. From here they were taken to the prison surgeon, who would record basic details like their height and weight, and any distinctive identifying bodily marks. His task was also to check whether the prisoner was insane (or had a family history of insanity) and certify to the governor that they were free from contagious disease. The preliminaries over, the prisoner would be taken to the reception ward – the part of the prison reserved for newcomers. As the inmate entered their cell a warder solemnly read out the prison rules before the doors were shut. The cells, whether in the reception ward or elsewhere, were all broadly similar. They measured about 12 feet long by 7 feet wide, were flagged with huge paving stones and roofed by a brick vaulted ceiling. The cells and the corridors that led to them were all carefully whitewashed with a special prison mix that had some soot in it to take off the white glare. Each arm of each pentagon had up to fifteen cells, whose windows looked out on to the central exercise yards and whose double doors opened on to the corridor. The windows of the cells faced a central circular

Millbank Penitentiary seen across the river Thames from Lambeth.
Its enormous size and forbidding walls and turrets must have made
a terrifying impression on new inmates arriving by river.

watchtower in the centre of each pentagon so they could remain
under constant surveillance. The inner door of each cell was of
reinforced wood with a vertical letter-box slit for warders to look
through; the outer door was made of iron bars. During the day the
inner door was left open, but at night both were carefully locked.
The prison was heated and lit by gas, and so pipes ran the length of
the corridors, feeding lights and burners that introduced warm air
into the cells. Special care was taken to ventilate the cells and a
grating in each ceiling allowed 'foul vapours' to escape.

The cells were sparsely furnished with a table, a stool, a bucket
for washing, and a hammock. Part of the daily routine was untying
and rolling up the hammock and neatly folding the blankets and
sheets with five symmetrical folds. On top of the folded bedding
the prisoner had to place his nightcap. On the table there was a
small pyramid of edifying books. Obviously there was a Bible,
Prayer Book and hymn book, but there were also religious tracts
and normally a book on arithmetic or another secular subject. To

aid study a slate and chalk were provided, and to encourage personal hygiene a comb, hairbrush and bar of soap. Each prisoner also had his own eating utensils: a bowl, a wooden plate and two mugs, one for cocoa and the other for gruel. Finally, beneath the table was stored a brush for cleaning out the cell. On the otherwise bare walls hung a card known as the 'Scripture Card' containing suitably reforming verses from the Bible and a 'Notice of Convicts' – the rules of the house. A remarkable refinement was the provision of a signal-wand for each cell. This was an ingenious device that allowed prisoners to summon a warder. By pushing one end of a metal wand through a slit in the wall the inmate could lift either a red flag for emergencies or a black one for less urgent requests.

This was all revolutionary. In comparison to what had gone before, prisoners at the Penitentiary were treated like kings. In fact the cell might, for many prisoners, be better than what they were used to at home, where they may have shared a room with half a dozen others in filth and cold. Yet, even in those appalling conditions, they had their liberty and were not subjected to the discipline, routine and relentless moralizing of the prison. Some of the most violent and angry prisoners reacted to the austerity, monotony and intrusiveness of the regime by insubordination, violence or even mutiny. They were sent to another class of cell known as the refractory cells. These were the punishment cells, one on the top floor of each pentagon, where the difficult prisoners were brought down by solitary confinement. Their windows were tiny, letting in only the minimum of light. There was no furniture, other than a stone and iron bed designed to be as unforgiving as possible. In these cells the wooden door was on the outside and the iron grating inside to increase the sense of isolation.

The refractory cells were psychologically devastating. The almost complete darkness, drastically reduced rations and no heating drove many prisoners to the brink of madness. When they were released, sometimes after many weeks, they were quite literally hospitalized. The prison infirmary was for them, and for others who fell sick of natural causes. It was laid out much like a modern hospital ward, with rows of beds hung round with curtains. There was a large

A nineteenth-century print of a prisoner in a refractory (solitary confinement) cell at Millbank.

bath at the entrance to ensure that inmates who were admitted were specially clean.

For the system of reform to work the prisoners had to have their minds reprogrammed. There were two aspects to this: religion and education. The prison chapel was in the centre of the prison, both geographically and conceptually. Prisoners had to attend each morning to sing hymns and listen to a sermon in silence. The continual reminder that they were particularly sinful and that Christ could take their sins away was delivered with a conviction that must have been overwhelming on a daily basis. There were also daily lessons. Attached to each pair of pentagons was a schoolroom with a blackboard, sloping desks and benches. The walls were covered in large maps and a series of charts showing the chronology of the Bible and the story of Creation. In the latter the central image was a picture of a man contrasted with a whale, to remind prisoners that they were among the smallest of God's creatures. Lessons in here covered arithmetic as well as Scripture. After the mind had been exercised and developed it was the turn of the body. The six central courtyards of the pentagons were essentially exercise yards, divided by high walls into five smaller sections. In these exercise took place in relays, the first starting immediately after morning chapel. Physical exercise lasted an hour and prisoners spent three-quarters of that time silently walking round the yard in circles. For fifteen minutes they would work a large pump in the middle of the yard (lifting water to the roof-top tanks), or a mill for grinding corn.

Hard work was the other crucial component of reform. There were thus workshops for prisoners in between some of the pentagons and the hexagon. Tailoring was the most common labour, both in individual cells and in larger workshops. Leatherwork, such as belt- and shoemaking was also undertaken. Those who were too clumsy, short-sighted or arthritic to sew were given coir to pick. This mind-numbing activity was to provide the fibres for weaving coir sacking, another prison industry. Other tasks included making buckets, furniture and even cartwheels. In seven months of 1854 the inmates at Millbank made 24,145 military greatcoats, 414,266 biscuit bags for the Navy, 1,920 pairs of shoes, and wove 103,720 yards of sacking amongst many other items.

The signal-wands were used each morning for roll-call. At dawn warders would patrol the corridors, banging on each cell door. Prisoners had to push out their wands to show that they were awake and well. The day would start with emptying out their buckets and sweeping their cells into the corridors; after this prisoners would march to the kitchen to get their breakfast. Each pair of pentagons had a kitchen run by warder cooks assisted by prisoners, in which stood a row of coal-fired boilers with bright red copper lids. Each could take several gallons of broth: the ingredients were prepared

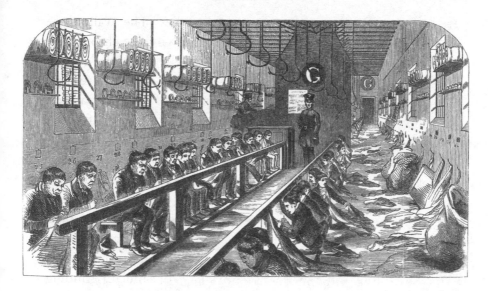

One of the workshops at Millbank after the prison had ceased to be
a reform penitentiary. Prisoners are stitching bags for the military
under the supervision of the guards.

on long dressers nearby. The floors were strewn with fresh sand.
Strangely it was diet that provided the first real controversy surrounding the Penitentiary. In February 1817, soon after the Penitentiary opened, to show how successfully the system was working,
the female prisoners were tested on their religious knowledge by
the Bishop of London, and everyone was very impressed by their
conduct. But this pious display hid an underlying rebellion. Many
of them were refusing their barley soup and were calling for a daily
increase of half a pound of bread. Soon complaints about the bread
were being heard throughout the prison, and some were refusing
to eat what bread they had. The rebels had in fact timed their protests
to coincide with a visit from the Chancellor of the Exchequer and
a group of his friends, who had planned to attend a Sunday service
at the chapel. On the Sunday morning the floors of the prison were
covered in bread hurled down the corridors by the angry inmates.
The governor, sensing danger, took 'three brace of pistols loaded
with ball' to his pew in the chapel. When the Chancellor and his
friends arrived the male prisoners banged the flaps of their kneeling

benches and pitched loaves of bread into the centre of the chapel and the women cried out, 'Give us our daily bread!' After the communion service had begun the women started screaming, 'Better bread, better bread!' At this the men rose up on to their benches but were cowed by the governor's waving pistol and resumed their seats. However the women carried on screaming until they were removed in small groups by officers, but not before six of them had berated the male prisoners' cowardly behaviour.

After the women's departure the service continued, and before he left the Chancellor of the Exchequer addressed the men, praising their restraint. The next day the governor went from cell to cell explaining that nothing could be done about the bread until the prison's management committee met. For some this was too much and they tried to stop their cell doors being shut, while others used their three-legged stools to beat on the woodwork, screaming and shouting. Four prisoners attacked a cell, smashing the furniture and the wooden door to pieces. The governor intervened but was attacked with a piece of door frame. The whole prison was in such uproar that the governor imported a band of Bow Street Runners (early policemen) and positioned them throughout the building. There was more trouble the next day, but the warders and staff managed to regain control of the prison the day after. The incident caused the governor to be sacked and the prison's reputation to sink.

Despite the bread riot, dietary provision for the prisoners was in fact extremely good. The amended prison diet consisted of a pound of bread for the whole day, a pint of hot porridge for breakfast, and on alternate days of the week their lunch consisted of six ounces of 'clods, stickings or other coarse pieces of beef without the bone' with half a pint of broth and a pound of well-boiled potatoes. On the other days they were given a quart of vegetable broth, thickened with scotch barley or peas, and a pound of well-boiled potatoes. For their evening meal they dined on half a pint of porridge. They were also allowed to save some of their lunchtime meal for supper. This was based on the well-tried diet used at Gloucester Penitentiary, but it rapidly became infamous for being far too generous.

The new Penitentiary was disparagingly referred to as 'the fattening house' and people joked that guards were employed more to keep people out than in. An Essex MP described the diet as 'an insult to honest industry' and 'a violation of common sense'. It should be said that the diet was too much for many inmates, and each day piles of boiled potatoes were wasted and fed to pigs. Soon the press got hold of the story, and eventually it was threatened that if the diet was not changed the Penitentiary might not have its licence renewed. Under ridicule and political pressure the prison authorities acted, and the diet was reduced. Under the new regime prisoners were only allowed soup. This was made from a broth made of boiled ox heads, which was divided between 200 prisoners, with peas or vegetables. It was rationed out in half-quart measures at lunch and supper. It was calculated that if the meat on an average ox head weighs eight pounds, each prisoner had the chance of consuming one and a quarter ounces of meat.

No one had considered the new diet with any care: its introduction was a reaction to hysteria rather than a careful reappraisal of what prisoners required. In fact it was said that 'what might have passed unnoticed in a far-off shire, was in London magnified to proportions almost absurd'. By the autumn of 1822 there were signs that something was wrong. A terrible lethargy descended on the Penitentiary: prisoners looked pale and weak, productivity in the workshops declined, laundry women fainted at their boiling coppers. By January the authorities were beginning to be very concerned and eventually a medical inspector discovered signs of scurvy. With this came diarrhoea and dysentery, accompanied by cramps, spasms and depression. By March the symptoms had spread throughout the whole prison, affecting half the population. The new arrivals were far less affected than the old-timers; men fared better than women; while many who worked in the kitchens were untouched. Importantly, none of the prison staff had any symptoms at all. Reluctantly the governor ordered the diet to be changed again. Now convicts were to enjoy a diet of four ounces of meat and eight ounces of white rice, white bread instead of brown bread, and three oranges a day.

The oranges cured the scurvy, but within a month a new epi-
demic had broken out, identified as 'the flux'. Now the whole
prison was affected with a kind 'of perpetual uneasiness within the
abdomen' accompanied by agonizing cramps, an irregular pulse,
twitching limbs, vertigo, and even in severe cases convulsions and
apoplexy. On 3 July the governor reported that 438 out of 800
prisoners were sick with the flux, and 30 had died.

This was a disaster. The governor was replaced, the diet was
changed again, but to little effect: during the summer the flux
spread to the staff. The only solution was to evacuate the prison.
This was a major undertaking, not only logistically but in terms of
the progress of penal reform. Emptying the prison was an admission
that the experiment was failing, or at least in peril. In August 1823
the male prisoners were taken from Millbank to Woolwich, where
they were put aboard hulks. Female prisoners, whom the reformers
did not want to see mixed in with the men on board ship, were
released on the basis that the flux had been punishment enough.
The men's health improved rapidly, although some later relapsed.
While the prison was empty Sir Humphrey Davy, chemist and
president of the Royal Society, was called in to examine the
buildings: he recommended complete fumigation with chlorine.
The moat, which had been filled with stagnant water, was connected to the Thames so the tides would clean it every day, and more
stoves were built in the corridors. The daily regime was changed
in order to increase the cheerfulness of inmates. There was now to
be a greater emphasis on exercise and more time was to be set aside
for schooling; controversially some of the books placed in cells
were now to be for 'rational amusement'.

The disastrous effects of disease were perhaps the most public of
Millbank's failures, but were far from the only ones. Discipline was
a problem right from the start, as the 1817 bread riots demonstrated.
Although the building was designed to subdue and reform, violent
protests and disturbances continued throughout its lifetime.

But despite the disorder this was a prison that was built to be the
ultimate in security. No prisoner was ever expected to be able to
escape its grim walls, guarded by watchtowers and a deep moat.

Yet numbers of prisoners did break free, the most successful of whom was Pickard Smith, who made a series of escapes in the 1830s. His most daring escape, which revealed the inherent weaknesses of the Penitentiary's design, was through the roof of his cell. He used a pin from the ceiling ventilator to scratch out the mortar from between the bricks in the ceiling vault. Soon, being accommodated on the top floor, he was through the ceiling into the prison's roof space. After finding a suitable weak spot in the slates, he made a hole through the roof before climbing down a rope made of bedsheets and clothes into the outer yard. There he found some boards and a ladder and made a ramp to effect his escape over the outer wall. Pickard was given up by his family but tried to escape five more times before being released. The free access prisoners had to tools and equipment assisted them in their escape attempts. One prisoner made a device for opening the bolt on his cell door through the warder's slot, and another inmate had used the heat of the gas lamp in his cell to fashion a key out of his pewter drinking mug. Yet escapes were not one of Milbank's most pressing problems: they merely reinforced the feeling that somehow this perfect building was a failure.

The only prisoners who were sent to Millbank and forced to endure this rigorous lifestyle were those who had the potential for reform. They had normally been given a commuted death sentence or been sentenced to transportation. They were also largely from the same social background as the prison population of today: the poor, the vulnerable, the dispossessed and the underprivileged. What is striking, however, is the youth of many of the prisoners and the seemingly trivial nature of their offences compared to the severity of their sentences. Charlotte Brown, thirteen years old, was charged with stealing pork and sentenced to seven years. An eleven-year-old Mr Braunch was charged with pocketing a child's necklace and sentenced to ten years. Others in their teens were imprisoned for stealing a handkerchief and a book, while a woman got eight years for stealing wet linen from a hedge. Although punishments were harsh, at the time it was often felt the Penitentiary was a far better place for children to be than out begging and stealing on the streets for their daily bread. This emerged when the prime minister, Lord Melbourne, came under attack in the House of Commons when Millbank was accused of unwarranted cruelty towards three girls and two boys in 1836. The allegation was that three girls aged seven, eight and ten, along with two boys, had emerged severely damaged after thirteen long and tortuous months in solitary confinement. On their release one had allegedly developed a stammer, another found it difficult to express thoughts, a third had developed idiocy, and one was so disturbed by the experience he was unable to break rocks. After an investigation it was revealed that in fact they had spent their days at Millbank exercising, attended lessons twice a week with chapel on Sunday, had been frequently visited by Christian ladies, and had left the Penitentiary in good health. Furthermore it was revealed that all the girls had been charged with stealing and had been sent to Millbank primarily to protect them from the influence of their parents.

The prison did have some better-off inmates. In the 1820s one observer noted that there were two captains, a baronet, four clergymen, a solicitor and a doctor behind the Penitentiary's bars. There was a surgeon, incarcerated for quadruple bigamy, a mayor in for fraud, a merchant serving time for forgery and a vicar with a gambling problem. A peculiarly interesting case was that of 'Mr P', a former army officer who attempted to strike the young Queen Victoria in the face with a cane as she left Buckingham Palace: he spent his time at the Penitentiary in relative luxury at the behest of the Home Secretary, until he was sent to Australia.

By 1840 disorder, epidemics, high mortality, escapes, child-scandals and a stream of inmates driven insane made the brave new world that the Millbank Penitentiary had hoped to usher in look very tarnished. In 1840 the medical journal the *Lancet* reported that 'the situation at Millbank penitentiary is bad . . . it has been shown by incontrovertible statistical facts, that imprisonment now destroys ten times as many lives as the executioner in this country'. Political confidence in the experiment had been fatally undermined. A series of changes of governorship accompanied by changes in the prisoners' regime had done nothing to address the problems. And this embarrassing disaster lay just up the river from the Houses of Parliament. In 1843 a comprehensive report was made on the prison and it was decided that the experiment had, in fact, been a complete failure. There was no evidence that the Penitentiary was actually reforming anyone; indeed quite the reverse in many cases. In addition it had been very expensive. The capital construction costs had worked out at about £300 a cell in 1829, and it cost £30 to keep a prisoner there for a year. The annual running costs for the entire jail were over £16,000. This was a vast expense compared to many other prisons, and unsupportable given the poor results.

An Act of Parliament in 1843 repealed Millbank's position as a reform penitentiary. The experiment was over and the great building officially a failure. Henceforth it would be used as a transportation depot. During a nine-month confinement prisoners would be assessed: some would be sent for reform elsewhere, others would be transported to Australia from the jetty in front of the prison's front door. In 1870 Millbank became a military prison and in 1890 it finally closed its doors. After lying empty for ten years it was demolished and the site used for the construction of the Tate Gallery. Today little survives on Millbank to show that the great prison was ever there. A capstan still stands by the river where the steam tugs that conveyed prisoners to the transportation ships tied up. In a housing estate behind the Tate there are the only remains of the ditch that once surrounded the prison, now used as a place for the occupants to hang out their washing. And a careful eye can trace in property boundaries the great hexagon that confined the penitentiary.

Why, though, did Millbank Penitentiary end up being classed as a failure? Was it the building or was it the regime that the prisoners were subjected to?

Undoubtably there were major problems with the design. Its plan was crazily large and confusing. Even the warders found it impossible to find their way about. Every corridor looked the same and changed direction every twenty yards; levels were connected with spiral stairs and linked by windowless passages. At each corner

After the prison ceased to be a reform penitentiary this engraving of the chain room was made. It shows the chains kept in the prison for restraining prisoners awaiting transportation.

was a gate and everywhere doors were locked: the potential for getting lost was high. One warder who had served for years at Millbank, and rose through the ranks to a senior position, carried with him a piece of chalk with which he marked his route, to help him work out where in the prison he was. This confusion was in stark contrast to more modern prisons, which were laid out much more simply.

The building's problems were not only in the plan. Another problem that dogged the design was sound transmission. The prevention of evil communications between prisoners had been one of the foundations of Howard's system. Unfortunately the ventilation gratings and the rigidity of the structure made it perfect for the transmission of sound, either by tapping or, more worryingly, simply by shouting. It was recognized that this not only weakened the principles of reform but made the prison very difficult to manage. Smirke was invited to build some experimental sound-proof cells, but they were as poor at keeping the sound out as the original ones. As a result a panel of distinguished experts, including the famous physicist Michael Faraday, were asked to design a soundproof cell. Twelve walls of varying specifications were built, tested and demolished between two cells. The favoured solution was a cavity wall filled with broken brick and canvas. It did not stop the noise, but it did reduce it to a meaningless mumble. Yet it was impossibly expensive to install such walls at Millbank. The entire prison would have had to be rebuilt. So although Pentonville Prison benefited from the Millbank experiments, the Penitentiary itself remained hopelessly noisy.

Then there is also no doubt that Millbank was a very unhealthy place, quite apart from the disastrous attack of scurvy followed by the (probably viral) flux. In 1854, while in use as a depot for transportation prisoners, the Penitentiary was included in a survey of London prisons. In this Millbank was found to have twice the sickness rate of any other prison: ten times the number of cases than at Pentonville, for instance. The low-lying dampness of the Thames side, and the water pumped from the river, were not conducive to good health.

Finally we have to wonder: was the prison actually just a plaything of the politicians and thinkers? It was next door to Parliament, and politicians, reformers and civil servants were forever visiting it. At the politicians' behest the prisoners' regime was continually being changed; a dozen reports and inquiries were launched. Was the Penitentiary Government vanity – an overblown and overfunded experiment intended to reflect well on politicians rather than addressing the true problems at hand? There may be something in this. It was built during very uncertain times. War with France had cost a staggering £800 million and had destabilized society and the economy. The French Revolution had shaken the British political establishment and there were great fears of a popular uprising. There had been harvest failure in 1811, Luddite vandalism in 1812, Corn Law riots in 1815. The State needed to bring order, discipline and religion back into society. In 1818 an Act of Parliament was passed to spend a million pounds in building new churches in London and elsewhere: fear of God and fear of the State were closely linked. Millbank can be seen as part of this reaction to disorder and social unrest: an investment by the Government in an experiment that might help restore confidence in the forces of law and order.

Tempting though it is to write the Penitentiary off as a failure, experiments which fail can be important. And Millbank was. The experiments in architecture and penal reform carried out there led directly to the new reform prison at Pentonville, opened in 1842. Pentonville was one of the most influential prison buildings in Europe and formed a blueprint for prisons all over the United Kingdom, many of which are still in use. Meanwhile the site of the great experiment is now home to another national institution, the Tate Gallery. An institution also dedicated to improving the mind and the spirit, but the medium for reform is not religion and hard work, but art.

Glastonbury Abbey

England's First and Last Monastery

Glastonbury is a place built on legend like no other. It is a place shaped and moulded by stories – some true, some certainly not, but as for most of them, we will never know. At its heart is the abbey, allegedly the oldest church in England and certainly by the time of its destruction in 1540 one of the two largest and richest. Glastonbury's remarkable history and its bloody end is the story of monasticism in England. It is the story of pride in place, a pride that came before a devastating fall.

Geologically the town of Glastonbury is a peninsula linked to higher land to the east and crowned with the pimple of sandstone that is the Tor. Before the surrounding watery Somerset Levels were drained it must have looked like an island, especially when approached from the west in a boat. For this reason from earliest times it has been the perfect place for secluded settlement whether as Avalon, the legendary hideout and death-place of King Arthur, or as a site for a remote religious community. The story goes that in AD 63 no lesser person than Joseph of Arimathea arrived by boat with twelve companions on a mission to spread the word of Christ. Weary from his travels he stuck his staff, fashioned from the branch of a thorn bush, into the earth, upon which it miraculously blossomed and took root. This was a sign both that his travels were at an end and that he should found a religious community on the island. With him, Joseph allegedly brought two powerful relics: the lance that pierced the side of Christ and the cup used in the Last Supper, which he had used to catch blood from Christ on the Cross – the Holy Grail.

It's a nice story, but try as hard as we might it is impossible to force the foundation of the present Glastonbury Abbey any earlier

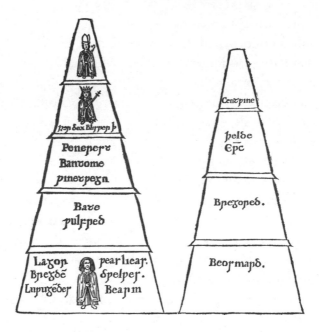

The pyramids or pillars of Celtic Glastonbury had long been demolished by the time Henry Spelman drew these reconstructions in the seventeenth century. They were probably 18–25 feet high and marked the burial places of the early abbots whose names and images appeared on them.

than the seventh century, when archaeological evidence begins to emerge of a permanent settlement on the site. Little is known about what the Abbey would have looked like then. However, until it was burnt down in 1184, the old church, or *vetusta ecclesia* as it was called in Latin, was highly revered as the oldest church in England, thought to have been founded by St Joseph himself. It originally lay where the ruins of the Lady Chapel now stand, built from timber planks with a thatched roof and measuring around 60 by 26 feet. William of Malmesbury, a medieval chronicler who visited the old church, mentions that 'pyramids' or stone totems inscribed with the names of its abbots stood outside it.

By the time of the Doomsday Book, Glastonbury Abbey was already the richest in England. The Normans brought no threat to that wealth, but ensured that for the first time it would be used to forcibly express the abbey's power in stone. The Norman Conquest was not only a political and dynastic revolution but also a religious one. William the Conqueror was determined that the Church would play an important role in the subjugation of the English, and used his patronage of bishops and abbots to bring both physical and spiritual servility to the new regime. He also harnessed architecture to meet his political ends. Not only were great castles and cathedrals built across England, stamping Norman authority on the Saxons, but the great abbeys were rebuilt too. For a century England became a massive building site. In fact in the eleventh century the Normans quarried as much stone for their projects as the Egyptians did for the construction of the pyramids.

In 1126 Henry of Blois, nephew of King Henry I, was appointed abbot. Now Glastonbury had one of the greatest figures of twelfth-century England at its helm, a man of taste, power and political skill. A man who went on to be the bishop of Winchester while still holding Glastonbury. A man who was one of the great builders of his age. And a man who was described by more pious and ascetic monks as the 'wizard of Winchester' or, less flatteringly, the 'whore of Winchester'. Henry of Blois created a building that we would recognize as a monastery today. There was the great abbey church, the architectural and spiritual centrepiece of Glastonbury. Then a cloister, nestled in the armpit of the church transept: it was used for exercise, conversation and study, and was in effect the monks' living room; their daily communal space. On the east side of the cloister there was the chapter house, the monks' boardroom, where abbey business was transacted. Then there was the dormitory, placed on the first floor with a warming-house beneath. Norman monastic dormitories did not have fireplaces, and monks would go to this room to warm up. The dormitory needed to be close to the abbey church to allow monks easy access for services at night – indeed, a special 'night stair' linked the monks' sleeping place with the choir of the church. At the end of the dormitory was the reredorter which contained latrines (or toilets) for the monks – their en suite facilities if you like. Nearby, around the cloister, would have been the refectory where the monks ate – probably on

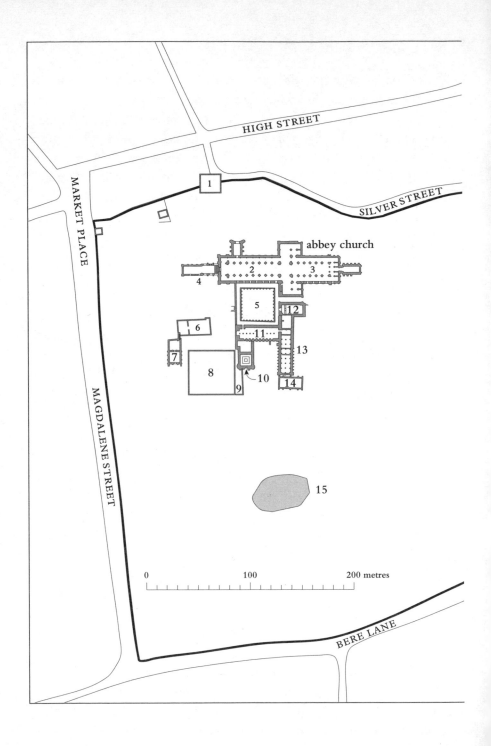

HIGH STREET

SILVER STREET

MARKET PLACE

1

abbey church

2   3

4

5

12

6   11

7   13

8   10

9   14

MAGDALENE STREET

15

0   100   200 metres

BERE LANE

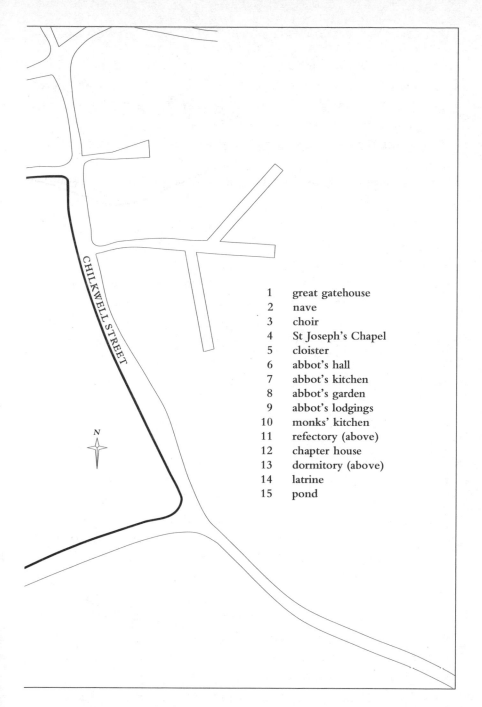

1	great gatehouse
2	nave
3	choir
4	St Joseph's Chapel
5	cloister
6	abbot's hall
7	abbot's kitchen
8	abbot's garden
9	abbot's lodgings
10	monks' kitchen
11	refectory (above)
12	chapter house
13	dormitory (above)
14	latrine
15	pond

Plan of Glastonbury Abbey at the dissolution in *c*.1539. Based on excavations and the surviving remains, this is as accurate as it is possible to get with the present state of knowledge.

the first floor in imitation of the site of Christ's Last Supper, which was held in an upper room; near this was the kitchen. Finally there was the abbey infirmary, a hospital and hospice for ill and dying members of the community. In addition to the monks' quarters there was a separate suite of lodgings for the abbot, including his own hall and kitchen.

Up to this point, although the history of Glastonbury had had its ups and downs, the story of the abbey had been one of mounting success, but the year 1184 was to be a turning point. On 25 May a ferocious fire tore through the old church and destroyed more or less the entire abbey. Only a couple of newer buildings remained, looking down on the rubble and ashes. This was a cataclysm, not principally because the priceless vestments, jewelled crosses, books and relics had been burnt, but because Britain's oldest church, the landing place of Joseph of Arimathea and one of the holiest places in Christendom, had been destroyed. The monks regarded this with double horror. Their reputation, their pride and their fame had been tied to the *vetusta ecclesia*. Without this visible sign of their antiquity Glastonbury was like any other abbey. Henry II immediately gave permission for the abbey's entire income to be directed towards the rebuilding of the church. But what would the monks commission for the sacred spot where the original church had stood?

Here we have a mystery. The chapel built to replace the *vetusta ecclesia* looks, from the outside, Norman (or Romanesque, to use a term that has Europe-wide significance). In other words it is based on round-headed arches and all the decorative motifs familiar from Norman churches and cathedrals: zigzag dog-tooth decoration around the windows; plain arcades on the outside. Inside, however, it is a different story. Suddenly, even today, one is in a Gothic building, an interior of pointed architecture. It was originally vaulted in Gothic stone vaults, and the details are all in the very latest French Gothic style of the mid 1180s. The monks had com-missioned a building that was in the very latest style inside but was in a style of the previous generation outside. Why?

Historians will argue over why this was so, but to me there seems

St Joseph's Chapel from the south as it appeared in the mid nineteenth century. It was built in a deliberately old-fashioned style, probably in imitation of the ancient church destroyed by the fire of 1184. It was consecrated in 1186.

a simple and convincing argument. The *vetusta ecclesia* was their most important asset, famous throughout England. How could they rebuild the oldest church in the land in a modern style? The antiquity, the dignity and the power of romance would have been destroyed. So the monks commissioned a building that deliberately looked old. A building that faked its age so as to impress visitors to the abbey. It was instant antiquity, instant credibility.

Inside it was a different story. The monks set out to dazzle. Both the architecture of the space, using seven different types of stone, and the colours used created one of the richest interiors of the twelfth century. It was overwhelmingly rich, a far cry from almost any comparable interior surviving today. The monks principally used blue and red, the blue made from lapis lazuli, a stone often more expensive than gold. To find a surviving parallel we need to go to a decorative arts museum – the Victoria and Albert Museum in London, for instance. Go to the medieval galleries and find the early medieval reliquaries – little jewelled caskets made of enamel, often in Limoges. These are usually decorated with architectural motifs in glowing Technicolor. Here you have St Joseph's Chapel* at Glastonbury in miniature. It was, in fact, a reliquary, a precious box designed to receive the most sacred relics available. But what would the monks put in it?

Before we address this vital question we need to turn to look at the whole notion of relics. Before the Reformation put an end to it all in England and Wales, corpses, skeletons, bits of bone, teeth, clumps of hair, pieces of skin, fingernails, vials of blood, shreds of cloth, splinters from the true Cross and piles of earth from places Jesus had been all had the power to consecrate an altar and intercede with God on behalf of a worshipper. These were the relics of dead saints, Christian martyrs, founders of churches and monasteries, pious kings and Christians, along with any earthly objects they may have touched during their mortal lives. They had universal powers, from curing disease to producing bumper crops. They could protect against every conceivable danger, from falling off a horse to being killed in battle. While, strictly speaking, to be effective the recipient of the favour had to worship at the shrine of the saint's relic, the power generally extended out to the whole region in which they were placed. But their protective force could be taken away in a frightening ritual of humiliation, by which the relics were arranged on the ground, covered in thorns, and the candles of their church extinguished. The validity of a relic rested on its ability to create miracles. A pile of earth taken from the spot where Jesus ascended to heaven, for instance, was believed to be real only if it caused a supernatural cure or miracle.

It was common not only for different monasteries and churches to contain relics of the same saints, but to claim to hold identical objects. In many cases this was accepted as part of the relic's ability

---

* The chapel was dedicated to St Mary and is now correctly known as the Lady Chapel, but it was historically and popularly known as St Joseph's Chapel. I will call it St Joseph's Chapel here.

The interior of St Joseph's Chapel. The scar of the pointed Gothic vault can be seen over the west window. The Gothic arcading beneath was painted in the richest colours, traces of which still survive.

to self-replicate, so that shrines and altars scattered across Europe housed identical remains. If all the pieces of the true Cross had been assembled, a clever joiner would have had enough wood for Noah's ark, and if the phials of Christ's blood had been pooled a significant blood bank could have been formed. However, disputes often arose as to which church or monastery had the actual relics of a local saint. For instance, there was a long-standing dispute

between Glastonbury and Canterbury over the remains of
St Dunstan, who in the tenth century had been abbot of Glastonbury but died as Archbishop of Canterbury. These disputes spawned
both a legitimate trade and a black market in authenticated relics
across Europe.

Relics were not simply spiritual status symbols: they were vitally
important both for establishing a consecrated church and for securing ongoing patronage, renown and pilgrimage. Pilgrimage was
particularly important because it brought revenue. Unfortunately
little is known about the income Glastonbury gained from pilgrims,
but it is known from records elsewhere that on average each pilgrim
would offer one penny. So the shrine of Edward the Confessor at
Westminster Abbey in 1360 received 21,600 pilgrims, bringing the
abbey £90 in revenue, and in 1190 the shrine of St Thomas à
Becket at Canterbury Cathedral saw 108,000 pilgrims, bringing in
£450. As well as offerings, profits also came from selling candles
that could be lit at shrines, and from souvenir stalls set up nearby,
where pilgrims could buy badges and other mementoes of their
visit.

We can be in no doubt about the spiritual and economic importance of relics to medieval monasteries, but what of Glastonbury's
collection? Most evidence of the vast number of relics kept at
Glastonbury comes from the abbey inventories. From the Old
Testament there were bits of Moses' and Aaron's rods, a piece of
Isaiah's tomb, and some relics of Daniel. From the New Testament,
there were several fragments of the Cross and some of the ground
where it stood, some of the stones where Christ was standing when
he ascended to heaven, a scrap of his tunic, and some whiskers of
St Peter's beard. Among the relics connected to the Virgin Mary
was a dribble of her milk – a particularly ingenious relic, since her
body was believed to have been transported intact directly to
heaven. This particularly spurious item was perhaps akin to the
foreskin of Christ, which at least twelve shrines in Christendom
purported to honour. Glastonbury also claimed to have some of
St John the Baptist's bones and bits and pieces from the Apostles
and holy martyrs.

Most of these treasures were destroyed in the fire of 1184, so the abbey was faced with the challenge of acquiring new ones for its beautiful jewel-like chapel of St Joseph. They had some early 'luck' and discovered, the very year of the fire, some fine relics of St Patrick, St Bridget and St Dunstan. However, with the death of their patron Henry II and the indifference of his heir, King Richard the Lionheart, they had to come up with something particularly powerful. In doing so they may have been inspired by the example of Canterbury. There, in 1174, there had also been a devastating fire, but the martyrdom of Thomas à Becket in 1170 had created a magnetic attraction for pilgrims and the entire rebuilding of the church was funded on the back of St Thomas's reputation. Glastonbury's traditional sacred founders were St Joseph, St Patrick and St Dunstan, (the latter Canterbury also had a rival claim to), but these figures were not attracting the attention required to fund the kind of building programme the abbey so badly needed.

On 29 March 1187, Constance, the widow of King Richard's younger brother Geoffrey, gave birth to a son, and with the King's permission was allowed to name him Arthur. Three years later on 11 November, just before the unmarried and childless King embarked on a crusade, he named Arthur as his heir. The scene was set for Glastonbury to make another discovery.

Armed with secret intelligence, the abbot of the day, Henry de Soilly ordered his monks to dig a hole between the two tall Saxon pillars next to the new chapel of St Joseph. Soilly claimed that an ancient Welsh bard had said that they would find the body of King Arthur 'at least sixteen feet beneath the earth, not in a tomb of stone, but in a hollow oak . . .' When and how this information was conveyed to the abbot is unclear, but exactly as the Welsh bard had predicted, sixteen feet down were found some very remarkable relics, the skeletons of a man and a woman. The man's bones were apparently enormous, and his head showed signs of being viciously attacked; the woman's bones were nearby and with them lay a truss of yellow hair, which crumbled into dust when an over-enthusiastic monk greedily grabbed it. Above the bones on the oak coffin lay a stone, on the underside of which was a lead plate in the shape of a

This lead cross was said to have been found in the grave of 'Arthur' in 1191. The script is late twelfth century, helping to confirm that it was a blatant fake. The original is now lost.

cross. It read: 'Here lies buried the renowned King Arthur with Guinevere his second wife, in the Isle of Avalon'.

Abbot Soilly had unearthed the ultimate relic. No one else had a piece of King Arthur, and few could claim to have such a pedigree for their relic, even down to a label.

It is easy to scoff at this extraordinarily convenient discovery, especially given the abbey's pressing need to boost its rebuilding fund and re-establish its dented ancient credentials. Yet all the evidence is that it was taken seriously – if not immediately, certainly in the long term. In 1278, nearly a hundred years after the original discovery, King Edward I and Queen Eleanor arrived at Glaston-bury. In the presence of the royal couple the graves of Arthur and Guinevere were opened and the bodies removed. The next day, in an extraordinary ceremony, the King wrapped the relics in precious cloths and reburied them in an enormous black marble tomb supported by four brass lions. This was placed prominently in front of the high altar, with the following inscription: 'Here lies Arthur, the flower of kingship, the kingdom's glory, whom his morals and virtue commend with eternal praise.' Arthur and Guinevere's knee-joints were then placed on top for the public to see.

The placing of a royal tomb in front of the high altar had enormous symbolic value. This position was normally reserved as the burial place of the founder of the abbey, so by building the tomb in this position the monks were clearly and very publicly claiming Arthur as the royal founder of Glastonbury. Professor Philip Lindley of Leicester University has suggested that if we want to visualize Arthur's tomb we need to look closely at the tomb of King Alfonso VIII of Aragon and Castile in the monastery of Las Huelogs in Burgos, Spain. Alfonso was married to the English Princess Eleanor Plantagenet, daughter of Henry II. Their joint tomb is supported by lions, contains a depiction of the king, an image of the Crucifixion, and is inscribed with a large cross on the lid. Arthur's was identical except it had a single roof rather than a double one.

While Arthur was the centrepiece of the new abbey church at Glastonbury, it soon filled up with other, lesser relics. The chronicler John of Glastonbury gave a vivid description of the relics there in the fourteenth century: 'The stone pavement, the sides of the altar, and the altar itself are so loaded, above and below, with relics packed together that there is no path through the church, cemetery or cemetery chapel which is free from the ashes of the blessed.' An enormous guidebook, the *Magna Tabula*, was created, measuring around 3 feet 8 inches by 21 inches. This was placed on a frame in the church, to be read by visitors. It gave a synopsis of the legend of St Joseph, and the stories of King Arthur, St Patrick and St Dunstan.

St Joseph's Chapel may have been the most important part of the new abbey that rose after the fire of 1184, but it was certainly the smallest. Work continued almost without a break for the following 350 years on completing and improving the abbey church and the abbey buildings. The monks lived on a perpetual building site,

The tomb of King Alfonso VIII of Aragon and Castile in the monastery of Las Huelogs in Burgos, Spain. Although this tomb is a double one, Arthur's tomb at Glastonbury would have been very similar – resting on lions, and made of black marble.

with hundreds of masons, joiners, plumbers and labourers at work every day. The abbots were men of God, but also businessmen and patrons of architecture. Much of their time must have been spent with the master masons who designed the new church, and the sculptors and carvers who embellished it.

The rapid completion of St Joseph's Chapel gave the monks a place to worship, to display their relics, and to welcome pilgrims and benefactors. They must have moved into temporary timber-framed domestic buildings themselves. The new church was then begun, starting at the east end. This was normal practice and would allow the parts that were most important liturgically to be finished first. The building of the new church then moved westwards until eventually in 1322–4 the great church joined up with St Joseph's Chapel in the west. This method of building meant that the monks must have decided on the vast scale of their building and its broad plan when they began, in 1184. As they laid the foundations of the east end, St Joseph's Chapel was still 550 feet away to the west. The gap in between was a football pitch and a half in length. This was staggeringly ambitious, even for an abbey as rich as Glastonbury. Winchester Cathedral is the longest church in England, and, remarkably, Glastonbury Abbey only falls short of it by six feet.

So what do we know of who designed the abbey and of the workmen who built it? Abbots and their monks did not design abbeys. Of the 12,000 craftsmen working in England from the Norman Conquest up until the end of Henry VIII's reign, only a handful may have been churchmen, and none were monks. It was the master mason, very often anonymous in the annals of history, who acted as architect, engineer, and frequently contractor too. Knowing as much as we do about the ambition, the scale, the cost and the ultimate success of these massive building operations it is all the more frustrating that we know little or nothing of their master masons. But we should not imagine that because these men lived up to six hundred years ago they were very different from modern architects. One medieval preacher used the image of a master mason to typify a snobbish professional who did little real work, visiting the masons' yard beautifully apparelled and haughtily drawing a line on a block of stone before ordering the masons to 'cut it for me so'. A criticism that some might make of architects today. Master masons, however, received a practical training in the masons' yard, an education which was every bit as much engineering as architecture.

We know of Adam de Northampton, who was appointed master mason at Glastonbury on 9 June 1253, with responsibility for the abbot's other works as well as the abbey church. He was obviously a much valued man. He was given a house, a pension for life worth 1s 8d a week and 13s 8d at Christmas for clothes. This scale of reward continued for the abbey's subsequent architects. Robert Lengynour was master mason for at least nineteen years. He was given the post for life by Abbot Geoffrey and was paid £8 a year and 20 shillings at Christmas for his robes. Every day he was entitled to bread, ale and cooked food from the abbey kitchens worth 5 pence, and each year his horse was to be provided with four wagon-loads of hay worth 10 shillings. Like Adam de Northampton he seems to have had a good pension too.

These are the men we know of, but there were others, handing down knowledge of Glastonbury and the great master plan for its completion from generation to generation, for a hundred years. They would have been responsible for drawing plans, sections and elevations for their masons and carpenters. Smaller drawings were on parchment, larger ones were made on tracing floors, large areas of smooth plaster that could be scrubbed clean for the next drawing to be made. Very often the drawings would have been translated into full-scale templates made of wood, or sometimes stone, for use on site.

Once the design was settled materials had to be gathered. Quarries were opened and forests identified for timber. Stone was Glastonbury's principal material. The cost would have been around twopence a cubic foot and a ton would have cost about 2 shillings, but this was nothing compared to the cost of moving it. Until the coming of the railways, potentially the largest cost of any building operation was the cost of transport. To move stone from the quarry to the abbey would have cost about twopence per ton per mile, which meant that over twelve miles the cost of the stone was equal to its carriage. However, Glastonbury owned its own quarry of high-quality limestone about twelve miles away at Doulting, just beyond Shepton Mallet, and as the abbot had manorial rights over the land between the quarry and the abbey, his tenants would have been obliged to cart the stone free, even repairing and building roads for its transport if need be. As a consequence expenditure at Glastonbury would have mainly gone on quarrying, designing, assembling and carving, rather than transport. Another regional limestone, blue lias, was used for all the finer work, such as subsidiary pillars and some capitals. Polished up, it could have the appearance of Tournai or Purbeck marble.

Just as the abbey owned its own quarries, it had its own woods – 6,000 acres of them. Building an abbey required very tall, straight trees, which are only found in mature forests. These produced beams for the roofs and smaller poles for scaffolding. The wood would have been cut into usable sections where it was felled, to avoid carrying unnecessary weight that would end up as offcuts or shavings. Usually the carpenters would prefabricate sections of roof in the forest before bringing parts to the abbey site for erection.

Other materials were more expensive: a ton of lead which could cover an area of roof measuring 160 square feet cost £2 to £3 between 1250 and 1350. There were lead mines in the Mendips and the monks of Glastonbury may well have used these for their roofs and pipes. A reliable water supply was vital for the existence of the abbey. Henry of Blois introduced the Roman plumbing technology used in France. The abbey's plumbing was a highly technical operation, on an industrial scale. There were probably only a handful of plumbers in England capable of designing and installing the water system at Glastonbury. Pipes were made in 20 foot lengths of rolled lead, and by decreasing their internal diameters water could be forced to travel under pressure. Water was piped from a covered spring first to the infirmary, then through the cloister lavatory to the kitchen and on to the brewery, where it was boiled, coloured and used for ale.

The most expensive material at Glastonbury was bronze. The average person may have had around two ounces of bronze in jewellery, or clasps and buckles, whereas an abbey bell weighed around two tonnes, or 64,000 ounces. The cost of the bell alone would have equalled the cost of the tower in which it hung. Because of their brittle structure, bells were usually cast on or very near to the tower itself.

To carry out building works on this scale the monks probably employed around 100 to 150 masons on a semi-permanent basis on a wage of around 4 pence a day. Employment by monasteries would have suited craftsmen as a more reliable form of income than work for the nobility, who often depended on royal favour for their building projects. The builders working for the abbey would prob-ably have also worked within a twenty- to thirty-mile radius of it in the surrounding countryside, while the master masons could have worked on a number of projects at once, at various locations on the abbey's lands.

Glastonbury continued to be embellished and improved until the reign of Henry VIII. By this time the Glastonbury monastic precinct would have been like a busy town within a town. In contrast to today's tranquil landscaped ruins, there would have been barely a blade of grass: most of the area would have been covered by yards and buildings housing light industries and agricultural processes, surrounded by ponds, watercourses and roadways. The monastic precinct itself was surrounded by the town of Glastonbury, as today, itself busy and bustling, full of traders and pilgrims.

Glastonbury was a Benedictine monastery, that is to say it followed a set of rules laid down in the sixth century by St Benedict. Over the centuries these rules were refined, and the very simple communities that St Benedict had envisaged became complicated businesses with enormous assets. In some respects the big monasteries like Glastonbury were run like a modern company. The abbot was the chief executive, with all sorts of perks and privileges, and a big budget for entertainment. Under him was the board of directors, in a monastery known as the obedientaries. These senior monks were in charge of the day-to-day running of the abbey. For instance, the cellarer was in charge of procuring the abbey's food and drink; the chamberlain was responsible for providing clothing and bedding; the infirmarer oversaw the infirmary or sick-house. The most important of the obedientaries was the prior, who was the abbot's deputy and was in charge of discipline in the abbey. Monks who did not hold office were known as choir monks; they were responsible for carrying out the daily round of prayers.

To enter the community a monk would take lifelong vows: chastity, poverty, obedience to the abbot and to the Rule, and the vow of stability (a commitment to stay in the monastery until death). He was allowed to leave the boundaries of the monastery if his work necessitated it but otherwise he was to stay within them, only opening its doors to the needy. The purpose of entering a monastery was to perform the *opus Dei* or work of God: this was done through a round of daily services in the abbey church. At the heart of these was the Book of Psalms, which was recited once a week by the monks. In the early Norman period the day of a monk

Ruins of the abbey church from the east, showing its extreme length.

would start at about two o'clock in the morning when, already fully clothed, he would feel his way down the night stairs connecting the dormitory to the abbey church. From then until about seven in the morning (with a few short breaks) the services of matins, lauds and prime would keep him in the abbey church at his psalter. After prime there would be an hour or so for reading and time to wash before returning to the church for the services of terce and, importantly, the first Mass of the day. After this a half-hour meeting in the chapter house would address matters of business and discipline. It was only half past nine when the monks were free to go out and undertake whatever work they had been assigned to do. By this time a monk would already have been up for seven and a half hours.

At about 12.30 the monks would return to the abbey church for the next service, sext, which was followed by the principal daily celebration of Mass. After this came their fifth service of the day, none. By this time it was about 3 p.m. and the monks would finally process to the refectory, where they ate dinner. Apart from their time in church, their day was conducted in silence. This included mealtimes, when one of their number would read out prayers or verses from the Bible. In many monasteries an elaborate sign language developed which allowed the monks to communicate over their meal. After dinner until roughly five in the afternoon was their second period of free time to read or work, before they returned to the church for vespers. After vespers there was a short rest and a drink before the final service of the day, compline, was recited. After this the monks would go to bed.

What I have described was the rule of St Benedict as practised in the Norman period. During the later Middle Ages the harshness of the Benedictine rule softened. There was an inevitability about this. St Benedict wrote his rule between AD 530 and 540 in the Italian monastery of Monte Cassino. He enjoyed hot summers and mild winters: observing his rule in north Yorkshire, or even in Somerset in January, was a different matter. Moreover as the standard of living rose and everyone from peasants to courtiers began to enjoy better houses with more technology the monks were not to be left behind, especially as most came from well-off families used to a degree of comfort. So as time went on many aspects of St Benedict's rule went by the board. The notion that monks should be paid wages became common; many abbeys acquired guest houses in which monks could take holidays; and single cells were built to replace the dormitories where the monks had slept communally.

The motivation for joining a monastery varied from one man to another, but we should not doubt that some or many had a strong religious vocation; for others, though, it was a career. Becoming an abbot put one at the pinnacle of society, and ambition was no stranger to the abbey churches of medieval England. As the monks themselves spent most of their time in prayer and contemplation, either in the abbey church or in the cloisters, a large monastery like Glastonbury employed a considerable number of servants to undertake the hard work of running the business. For instance, most abbeys had their own bakehouse for making bread, a mill to grind corn and great barns to store grain. These would be managed by the monks but worked by secular servants.

By the late fifteenth century, while most of the large monasteries in England were maintaining the *opus Dei* in broad terms, the original vision of St Benedict was unrecognizable in them. Standards of living had risen and life in the great abbeys could not be considered remotely austere – monks were often overweight through over-indulgence and lack of exercise, and learning and devotion in some institutions had been allowed to slip. It was for this reason that reform was a subject of great interest. What started as reform of the purpose of monasteries got entangled in the reign of Henry VIII with something much more powerful, and much more destructive.

The religious crisis of the reign of Henry VIII is familiar, in outline, to most people. The whole business started with the genetic inability of Henry VIII to produce strong male children. His divorce of Catherine of Aragon and his marriage to Anne Boleyn was intended to solve the succession crisis but in the process caused a row with the Pope that triggered what we now call the Reformation and the dissolution of the monasteries. At the start of Henry's reign, in 1509, there were two parallel hierarchies across Europe, one established by the Church that answered directly to the Pope in Rome, the other answering to the king of each country. Technically the monarch derived his power to govern from God via papal authority. What Henry VIII seized upon was the merging of the two hierarchies, making himself supreme head of both Church and State in England and Wales. Henry's break with Rome was essentially done for self, and therefore national, interest, and the creation of a national Church did not mean it would necessarily be a Protestant one. But it did mean the appropriation of all the economic resources of the English Church which, as its head, were now rightly his.

The mechanism for both his assumption of supreme headship of the Church and the appropriation of Church wealth was Parliament, and in order to persuade Parliament to act, Henry needed a gifted agent. He found him in Thomas Cromwell, later made Earl of Essex. Cromwell was one of Cardinal Wolsey's chief assistants and on Wolsey's fall the King gave him the task of supervising royal business in what we now know as the Reformation Parliament

(1529–36). His brilliance shone and the King promoted him to Principal Secretary in 1533. From this point onwards until his execution on trumped-up charges of treason and heresy in 1540 he was the King's vicar general, realigning Church and state to cope with the massive changes that the Reformation and the dissolution of the monasteries brought. He was responsible for using his network of spies and henchmen to dismantle one of the major institutions of England. It was as if the government today had decided to abolish all supermarkets and take their land and assets for itself. Between 1536 and 1540 nearly 900 individual bodies were liquidated, displacing 11,000 people out of a population of approximately 2.8 million.

The first step was the passing of the Act of Supremacy in November 1534. This dissolved the age-old ties between Westminster and Rome, making Henry the head of the Church in England with powers to teach doctrine, order worship and reform the Church. The second step was the transfer of revenues from the papacy to the Crown, and this was made possible by an act of parliament known as 'First Fruits and Tenths', passed in November 1534. The first fruits, or more technically the 'annates', were the first year's revenues from any Church office and its lands. These had, since the thirteenth century, been passed to the Pope. The new Act transferred this lucrative revenue stream to the Crown. But there was a problem. The reckoning by which the value of a year's income was gauged dated from 1291 and was clearly out of date. As a consequence a royal commission under the Chancellor of the Exchequer, Sir Thomas Audley, and the Vicar General, Thomas Cromwell, was created to assess the wealth of every religious house and church in every parish of England and Wales. Each county had its own commission, normally chaired by a bishop and comprising local gentlemen and public officials such as mayors, justices of the peace and sheriffs.

Members of churches and monasteries, together with local officials, were obliged to appear before the commission and swear under oath that the information they had given was correct. Commissioners were ordered to draw up records of rents, farms, manors, mills and other secular revenues along with their religious incomes through local church tax in the form of tithes, and charitable gifts. This massive operation was executed at breakneck speed: commissions were established on 30 January 1535 and ordered to send their completed account books to London on 30 May. Although the rapidity of the survey seems reckless, the information required was relatively easy to gather, since monasteries kept meticulous accounts for the good running of their houses, and the commissioners, who were not paid, wanted to finish the work as soon as possible. Whilst the returns were in fact not completed until the beginning of 1536, it was still an extraordinary achievement which owed a great deal to the pressure from Cromwell to have it finished quickly.

The commissioners met with little resistance, since the major concern of churchmen was future tax avoidance. This anxiety, not surprisingly, ensured that the real value of Church assets was underestimated. Their reaction would have been quite different if they had foreseen that the survey was a prelude to the wholesale transfer of Church wealth to the Crown. The completed survey is now known as the *Valor Ecclesiasticus*, literally 'the valuation of the Church', and was an incredibly ambitious document, akin to the Doomsday Book in its scope and importance. Amazingly it continued to function as the official guide for the assessment of Church benefices for nearly four centuries, until they were finally abolished in 1926.

This massive twenty-two volume record gives us a picture of the monasteries on the eve of the dissolution. For Glastonbury there is even more information: in order to allow a careful analysis of the monastery's wealth, one of the royal clerks decided to take a complete set of recent abbey accounts (obedientiary rolls) back to London. These still survive today in the National Archives at Kew, where they have been carefully preserved for 450 years, and give us a snapshot of life at Glastonbury Abbey in its last days. The first thing to note is that the spiritual life of the abbey was certainly vibrant. There were fifty-five monks, eight of whom had joined in the previous four years. The accounts clearly show that Mass was frequently celebrated and that vestments were washed and repaired. Money was paid out for 1,100 pounds of candle wax, and wages were paid to priests for saying mass. Significant payments were also made to ensure a high quality of music: the abbey singing master was paid £10 a year for playing the organ at services and teaching six pupils.

Learning was not neglected either. Although the commissioners did not bother to value Glastonbury's books, we know that it had one of the most important libraries in England. When it was visited by the Tudor antiquarian and bibliophile John Leland, he was astonished by the treasures there: 'Scarcely had I crossed the threshold when the mere sight of the most ancient books took my mind with an awe or stupor of some kind, and for that reason I stopped in my tracks a little while. Then having paid my respects to the deity of the place, I examined all the bookcases for some days with the greatest interest.' Many of the books seen by Leland dated back to before the thirteenth century, when there were already 500 books. Some of them were commissioned by the abbey's famous abbots, such as St Dunstan, and at least thirty were of a pre-Conquest date. The library at Glastonbury was thus a very great centre of learning, and it cannot be doubted that it would have been in daily use.

The Abbey's economic position was excellent, too. It owned somewhere around 130,000 acres, with an estimated 2,800 tenants paying an average rent of 4s 6d per acre. This and other assets brought an annual return of £3,311 7s 4d, making it the second richest house in the land – only £270 a year worse off than Westminster Abbey, the burial place of monarchs and neighbour to the royal palace of Westminster. Glastonbury was thus, apart from Westminster, the richest in the land, richer even than the Archbishop's own cathedral at Canterbury.

But this wasn't all. Glastonbury's strongrooms and cupboards, its vestries and altars, were groaning with gold, silver and other priceless objects. The total value of the abbey's chalices, pyxes, monstrances and crucifixes is not known, but the gold alone totalled over 11,000 ounces. The abbey's vestments, woven with gold and silver thread, were worth £1,100. By comparison, Bury St Edmunds Abbey had 1,553 ounces of gold and Ely Cathedral Priory had 344. The wealth of Glastonbury outshone almost everywhere else.

The obedientary rolls also help us visualize the daily diet of the monks and their guests. This was dominated by the liturgical calendar – crucially, whether a day was a feast or fast day. For the feasts no effort was spared. Whether it was the anniversary of the foundation of the abbey church, Christmas, Easter or any of the other great celebrations, the kitchens pushed out the boat. Easter eggs on Easter day, six salted salmon on Lady Day and meat pasties on Corpus Christi. Figures for the last year of the abbey's existence show the supply of meat, fish and dairy produce. The meat comprised 176 oxen, 5 cows, 1 bull, 634 sheep, 52 calves and 284 pigs, probably eaten on ordinary days and feasts. The fish, generally eaten on fast days, comprised 2,183 shellfish, 3,243 hake, 8,532 herrings, 131 salmon and 30 eels. In addition there were 575 pounds of butter and 2,016 pounds of cheese. These supplies would have been cooked in two separate kitchens, one for the monks and the other for the abbot himself. The abbot's kitchen, with its four tall chimneys and pointed roof, is the only part of the abbey to survive intact. This building, dating from the mid fourteenth century, is square externally but octagonal inside, with huge fireplaces in each corner. Its great height helped keep the kitchen cool when all its hearths were burning. We know that in the last three months of 1538 90 oxen, a bull, 3 cows, 6 calves, 7 pigs and 144 sheep were roasted in here. Provisions were also ordered for the infirmary, where sick monks were given specially distilled medicinal cordials. Their diet was especially designed to aid recovery and included porridge, butter, milk, fresh fish, cheese and ginger.

All this amounted to an institution in its prime spiritually, intellectually, economically and socially. Indeed Glastonbury was in the forefront of a Benedictine resurgence of the sixteenth century. It, like the other Benedictine abbeys, had accepted the Act of Supremacy of 1534 which placed them under the authority of the Crown: there was no sense that the abbot or anyone in the monastery was anything other than loyal to the concept of an English

The abbot's kitchen, the most remarkable and well-preserved monastic kitchen to survive from the Middle Ages, and the only roofed structure to survive from Glastonbury Abbey today.

Church. The abbey was governed by a competent and professional abbot. It was economically self-sufficient (some might have said dominant) and a major centre of learning and scholarship; it played a very significant part in the spiritual life of the area and was a major patron of art and architecture. Many of its members would have come from families with connections and wealth. Some would have been ambitious to serve, in due course, in the hierarchy of the Church or the State.

In the summer of 1535 Cromwell sent out a second group of assessors to the monasteries. The first commission having gauged their economic value, this group was to gauge their moral and spiritual health. Bishops traditionally carried out 'visitations' of religious communities to check that they were still adhering to their founding principles and disciplines: any recommendations were usually delivered in confidence and only to the abbot. But under Henry VIII's new rules the Crown had powers to 'visit, repress, redress' and 'reform' the religious and Cromwell, as his vicar general, took the opportunity to select his own men for the job. The visitation was an enormous undertaking, considering the few men involved and the number of religious houses they visited. Within six months they had made their report, and in 1536 their scandalous findings were read out to Parliament, serving as a justification for what was to come. Letters to Cromwell from seven visitors survive. The most infamous of this group, for his inquisitorial manner and the crude anecdotes in his letters, was Richard Layton, a doctor of civil law who had worked for Cromwell for over a decade. Even before Cromwell had appointed the visitors, Layton was pushing to visit the north, where he had numerous relations. Accompanying him was another agent, Thomas Legh, a former ambassador to Denmark and a particularly unpleasant character. Disliked by the Duke of Norfolk and the French ambassador, he was arrogant, domineering, cold and humourless. Like Layton, he had been involved with the execution of Anne Boleyn. An extract from one of Layton's letters shows his contempt for both the clergy and the common people: 'There can be no better way to beat the King's authority into the heads of the rude people of the North than to show them that the King intends reformation and correction of religion. They are more superstitious than virtuous, long accustomed to frantic fantasies and ceremonies, which they regard more than either God or their prince, right far alienate from true religion.'

In four months, and in between other business, this opinionated man managed to tour a considerable area of the country: on 1 August he was at Evesham in Gloucestershire, then Bath, through Devon to Glastonbury, where he interviewed the abbot and toured the buildings. From Glastonbury he moved to Bristol, Oxford and Abingdon, then down to Winchester and up to Southwark, and back down to Hampshire. He then moved to Kent through Dover, Folkestone and Langdon, and by 23 October he had reached Christ Church, Canterbury. Around a week later he managed to journey to Rochester, and down to Bermondsey, completing his tour at Syon on 12 December.

This was fast, very fast, and it soon became clear that speed was the least of the problems. While the commissioners commended the good running of many religious communities and were willing to defend others threatened with closure, it was increasingly obvious that their aim was less to reform than to rapidly gather damning information for Cromwell. Layton and Legh seem to have taken great pleasure in bullying, intimidating and eliciting the sexual abuses of the monks and nuns. There were reports of monks and nuns breaking their vows of chastity, with 181 cases of sodomy between the monks (although in some regions 'solitary vice' was reported as sodomy, so the figures are unclear). The letters often read as catalogues of incriminating evidence against the monasteries, listing their abuses with no suggestion as to how they might be reformed. Layton visited Glastonbury on Saturday 21 August 1535 and wrote to Cromwell on the following Monday from Bristol. His report was glowing: 'at Glastonbury,' he wrote, 'there is nothing notable; the brethren be so straight kept that they cannot offend.' The great abbey at Glastonbury had passed the first test.

On 11 March, only a few weeks after the completion of Layton and Legh's whirligig tour, a bill came before Parliament to abolish (or suppress) the smaller monasteries worth less then £200 a year. This Act of Suppression resulted in the closure of around a third of all religious houses. A new 'Court of Augmentations' was established to deal with what was eventually to become the largest transfer of land in modern English history: the court was essentially a ministry for the nationalization of the Church.

The seizure of monastic lands and wealth and the subsequent closure of all of their houses took place in just four years: while the Act of Suppression closed the smaller houses a growing policy of pressure brought about the 'voluntary surrender' of the larger ones. And of these Glastonbury was the largest and richest, and Cromwell's men knew it. They wrote to him stating that Glastonbury was 'the goodliest house of that sort that ever we have seen . . . a house mete for the king's majesty and for no man else . . . The house is great, goodly and so princely as we have not seen the like; with 4 parks adjoining . . . a great mere . . . well replenished with great pikes, bream, perch and roach; 4 fair manor places . . . being goodly mansions.' Two things we can be entirely sure of: that Glastonbury was probably the richest, oldest and proudest abbey in England; and that Henry wanted it, every last rent, stone and carat of gold. There was one obstacle in the King's way, and that was its abbot, Richard Whiting, a man who had absolutely no intention of surrendering the abbey voluntarily.

Comparatively little is known of Whiting's life. He came from a distinguished family and it appears that his uncle was chamberlain at Bath Abbey. His immediate family was from the Wrington area, north of the Mendips. He probably went to Glastonbury's monastic school, and rose through the orders quickly after becoming an acolyte, and subsequently sub–deacon and deacon. He was ordained as a priest in 1501 at Wells. It seems likely that he was then made chamberlain of the Abbey, where his responsibilities would have included the dormitory, the lavatory, and the community's wardrobe. This role would have given him responsibility for numerous officials and servants.

A week after Abbot Bere's death in 1525 the forty-seven monks of Glastonbury met to appoint a successor and requested that Cardinal Wolsey select a distinguished prelate to be their head. Wolsey, on advice, decided on Whiting, who was praised as being 'watchful and circumspect . . . upright and religious . . . commendable for his life, virtues and learning'. When he heard of his election,

The chair of Abbot Whiting, today preserved at the Bishop's Palace at Wells, the site of Whiting's trial. Such chairs were symbolic of an abbot's status and were collapsible so they could accompany the abbot on his travels.

Whiting, presumably in a state of shock, rejected the offer and fled to the abbey's guest house followed by two other monks, who tried in vain to persuade him. Whiting called for time to pray and think. A few hours later he emerged and 'unwilling any longer to offer resistance to what appeared the will of God', accepted. By all accounts an unexceptional abbot, Whiting seems to have been an amenable and conventional man who enjoyed all the comforts of his position as head of the second wealthiest abbey in England.

Although there was no criticism of Abbey discipline and Layton thought well of the abbot, from August 1535 on the screw was gently but firmly turned on Whiting and his abbey. A series of royal regulations gradually made his life difficult, removing Whiting's powers over his estates and weakening his position within the abbey. Junior members of the community were encouraged to report senior members for perceived misdemeanours. An Orwellian atmosphere grew; no one could trust anyone else. Amidst all this, in 1538 the abbey was the subject of another visitation. It uncovered a hotbed of discontent. Allegations were made to the visitors of every kind of abuse. Services were too long, relics were not being honoured, the abbot had favourites, education was neglected, even the quality of the ale had collapsed. Glastonbury was imploding under royal pressure and its abbot was on the verge of a nervous breakdown.

But Whiting still believed the abbey could be saved, even though by early 1539 it was the only surving monastery in Somerset. Was Whiting behaving like an ostrich, or did he have a plan? We shall never know, for that summer the commissioners lost patience. Under enormous pressure from Cromwell, Layton was forced to take back his admiring report on Glastonbury of 1535. He now claimed that Whiting appeared neither then or now to have 'known God or his prince' and that although he had a fair outward appearance his thoughts were inwardly cantankerous. At the end of September Cromwell's three chief visitors returned to Glastonbury and found Whiting at the monastery's nearby manor house of Sharpham. They insisted on interviewing the exhausted and frightened abbot. Some interview it was. The interrogation insisted that he 'call to mind what he had forgotten and tell the truth'. Sharpham was thoroughly searched, but for what, no one was clear. The visitors' henchmen moved on to the abbot's lodgings in the abbey and to his study. There they unearthed a book of arguments 'against the divorce of the King's majesty' and several old papal pardons, together with a life of St Thomas à Becket. The life of Becket, the archbishop who defied his king, was taken to represent Whiting's treasonous state of mind. The abbot was bundled on to a horse and taken to the Tower of London.

This was all clearly a fix. The royal visitors had nothing on Whiting. What the book of arguments was is unclear, but the papal pardons and a life of Becket could be found in almost every church library in the land. The visitors were scraping the barrel. At the Tower of London Thomas Cromwell himself became the principal interrogator. There, Whiting confessed that he had hidden some of the Abbey's gold and silver from the King's commissioners. Cromwell added theft to the original charge of treason.

A man of the stature of Whiting would have, in the past, been tried by his peers in Parliament, but after April 1539 an abbot had no official status and so would be tried by a local court. Cromwell callously jotted down in his notebook, 'the abbot of Glason to be sent down to be tried and executed at Glaston'. Poor Whiting was extracted from the Tower and sent back to Somerset.

The last abbot of Glastonbury stood trial at the Bishop's Palace at Wells on 14 November 1540 before Lord John Russell. He was tried with common criminals by a jury 'very diligent to serve the King'. He was found guilty of robbing the abbey at Glastonbury of the King's gold and silver and condemned to death.

Richard Whiting was a man of the world as well as being a man of God. He was a businessman, a politician, a manager, and a man used to seeing justice and punishment handed down. He knew that condemned criminals and traitors were taken to their execution on a hurdle. A hurdle was a horse-dragged wooden framework, to which a condemned man was lashed. Not even in his worst nightmare could he have imagined that he, the abbot of Glastonbury, would ever be strapped to a hurdle. Yet on 15 November 1539, at the gates to the abbey, the old man was manhandled on to a hurdle and dragged through the town that had been his home for fifty years. With the abbot were two others: John Thorne, the abbey treasurer, and Roger Wilfred, one of the monastery's youngest members. The execution party struggled to the very top of the Tor, where three gallows were waiting. As soon as Whiting was dead he was taken down and decapitated. His body was then quartered and the parts sent to be displayed at Wells, Bath, Ilchester and Bridgewater, while his head was placed on a spike held aloft above the abbey gate.

In an age of brutality the execution of Richard Whiting seems particularly unforgivable. Why did Henry VIII make an example of this unfortunate old man? At the start of the process of dissolution Whiting, like many others, probably thought that the problem would simply go away. After four or more years of Cromwell's men poking into Glastonbury's business, the inquisitions of 1539 may have just seemed like more interference. Whiting, like many others, probably didn't take the issue very seriously until it was too late. There was also a possibility that he believed that the largest abbeys, like his own, would survive – perhaps even as universities or cathedrals. Glastonbury, after all, was the oldest religious community in the country, founded by St Joseph himself. In front of the high altar was buried England's most famous king, Arthur. Henry VIII's elder brother, who had died while still a boy, had even been named after Arthur; that the King would want to dissolve such a house was unthinkable. Whiting, like many of his predecessors, may have regarded its position as unassailable. If Whiting believed that it would never happen, Cromwell was determined that it should. But the question remains: why was it effected so brutally? Why force through the show trial and bloody execution of an old man? The answer is that in early 1539 England and Henry himself were facing an international showdown. Pope Paul III had decided to excommunicate Henry and was encouraging the Scots, French and Spanish to invade England and re-establish Catholicism. Henry was panicking and the whole country was on a war footing: defences were strengthened and troops were mustered. The last thing the King wanted was internal opposition, and Whiting's stand against royal authority might just have been enough to trigger a domestic rebellion such as the northern Pilgrimage of Grace that had taken place in 1536–7. The risk of internal opposition coinciding with an external crusade was too much to countenance. Whiting had to be removed, and quickly. The Dissolution, the Reformation and Henry's throne itself were at stake.

Glastonbury was the last monastery to fall into Henry VIII's hands, and so with the execution of Abbot Whiting English monasticism died. Glastonbury had been its birthplace and Glastonbury Tor was to be its monument.

This engraving by William Stukeley depicting the ruins in 1723
shows the monastic remains and the surviving abbot's lodging and
kitchen. The lodging seems to have been very comfortable, with
vaulted cellars and panelled rooms above.

So what happened to the great monastery when its abbot was
dismembered? As Whiting was being carted away to the Tower
the royal treasurers were hungrily stripping the abbey of its assets.
Cupboards were broken open, vaults prised apart and the abbey's
riches were disgorged. Work had already begun to strip the roof of
its lead, to prise the glass from the windows and rip the tiles from
the chancel floor. In one sense Glastonbury was unlucky. A small
minority of monastic houses were allowed to remain in the form
of cathedrals – Westminster, Canterbury, Winchester, Durham and
York, for example; but Glastonbury was too close to Wells for that
to be its saving grace. Others were granted to courtiers and turned
into mansions, like Laycock, Woburn or Syon. Glastonbury was
too rich for that fate: Henry wanted the wealth himself. So the great
abbey at Glastonbury became a building quarry. When Edward VI
granted its site to the Duke of Somerset ten years or so later, nothing
of value was left. Well, almost. Perhaps out of respect for the *vetusa*

ecclesia it alone remained, unroofed but otherwise intact. Perhaps even Henry VIII's henchmen had respect for the oldest church in the land; perhaps they too had fallen for the legends that the monks had so carefully nurtured.

The monks of Glastonbury were not as roughly treated as their abbot and his two colleagues. They were given pensions to live off by the Court of Exchequer. The average pay-out for a monk was £5 a year, which would have only provided subsistence. It was also assumed that monks would find employment in the Church to supplement their pensions, whilst many nuns decided to exchange their robes for married life. Twenty-five monks from Glastonbury were still receiving their pensions as late as 1555, when their names still appear on the Exchequer's lists.

The monks of Glastonbury carefully crafted, indeed faked, a history and an image for themselves. That image was certainly a factor in their abbey's downfall, but more importantly it was the key factor in its survival. The image of Glastonbury today is arguably more powerful than the reality was in the Middle Ages. Glastonbury is still a holy place, a mysterious place, and a place of myth and legend. It is a holy site for Christians, and the place of choice for hippies, New Age spiritual seekers and music festival fans. The abbey is visited by hundreds of thousands of visitors a year – many more visitors than there were ever pilgrims. This lost building is only lost in body: in spirit it lives on.

Postscript

Lost Buildings . . . Lost Britain?

We live in one of the most intensively occupied countries in the world: an island that has been settled by successive waves of invaders, refugees and traders. Each wave of occupation has modified what it has found. People have adapted and absorbed the best of the past to make their present work. The result of three thousand years of continuous change and development is the remarkable landscape we now live in. Our countryside is almost entirely man-made. The qualities that we appreciate in the Scottish Highlands, the Lake District or the South Downs are only natural in the loosest possible sense. These are landscapes that have been moulded by agriculture and recreation. Stone walls, copses, lanes, hedgerows, woods, ponds, lakes and watercourses have all acquired their present shape through our endeavour. More obviously, so have our villages and towns. Some have been settlements for thousands of years; a very few still have physical remains stretching back a millennium; and many thousands, at their core, are built around buildings 500 years old. In England alone there are 18,000 medieval parish churches, each one the centre of a settlement representing man's efforts to make a mark on the landscape.

These ancient buildings and landscapes are one of the most important components in our quality of life. The historic places around us give us a sense of history, a sense that the place in which we live is not anywhere, it is somewhere. It is what makes Manchester different from Bath and Northumberland different from Shropshire. It is why millions of tourists cross the globe to visit this island and why when they come here they are amazed and fascinated by the extraordinary depth of history they find.

But our historic environment is as fragile as our natural one. It is vulnerable to the elements, to neglect, to thoughtless, short-term development: it is always under threat and, crucially, it is not renewable. Once it has gone it has gone for ever. Historic character can virtually never be rebuilt or recreated. Once landscapes are scarred, over-developed or suburbanized; once the historic street patterns of towns are ironed out and mass-produced building materials overwhelm traditional ones, it is impossible to reverse the damage. Lost buildings are lost for good. When they are lost their influence may live on but the power they exert on our quality of life is destroyed for all time. That is why it is more important than ever before for twenty-first-century Britain to treat the modernization and development of our country with care: to think carefully before expanding our towns into the countryside, to quantify the effects of traffic schemes and in-town shopping centres on the character of our streetscapes.

Without this careful thought the relentless effects of mass production, traffic management and short-term economic gain will rub out the subtle distinctions that give this country its character. They will erase irreplaceable parts of our historic environment in a thoughtless and uncontrolled homogenization.

It can be stopped, but only if people show that they care. Too many local authorities suffer from a lack of self-confidence, a lack of civic pride and ambition, and perhaps a lack of skills too. In their eagerness to modernize, permission is given for development bringing short-term economic gain and long-term destruction of the historic environment. Valuable historic buildings are demolished, over-extended or disastrously altered, damaging the character of places and the quality of people's lives. It is therefore down to all of us to save what is important in our environment. It is our responsibility to ensure that historic buildings and sites that contribute positively to our lives, define the places where we live, and give us a sense of identity are preserved for the future. It is people-power that saves historic places, that preserves the sense of identity and place that we all value. No one is suggesting that we pay the price that Abbot Whiting of Glastonbury paid for attempting to defend a building that he believed was important, but it would be unforgivable if we didn't try to preserve what is so important to us.

Further Reading

I have not attempted to provide a complete list of books referred to, but rather to suggest where the interested reader can follow up some of the themes in this book.

Whitehall Palace

The definitive book on the archaeology of the east side of Whitehall is my own *Whitehall Palace: An Architectural History of the Royal Apartments 1240–1698* (Yale, 1999). Simon Thurley, *The Lost Palace of Whitehall* (London, Royal Institute of British Architects, 1998) and Simon Thurley, *The Whitehall Palace Plan of 1670* (London Topographical Society, 1998), cover my most recent thoughts on the palace as a whole. Per Palme, *The Triumph of Peace: A study of the Whitehall Banqueting House* (Uppsala, 1957) is out of print, but a brilliant and useful book on the Banqueting House. For life at the Tudor palace see Simon Thurley, *The Royal Palaces of Tudor England* (Yale, 1993). For James II see John Callow, *The Making of King James II: The Formative Years of a Fallen King* (Stroud, 2000) and John Miller, *James II, A Study in Kingship* (London, 1989). For more detail on the importance of the chapel see Simon Thurley, 'The Stuart Kings, Oliver Cromwell and the Chapel Royal 1618–1685', *Architectural History*, 45 (2002) pp. 238–74; and for the role of London in James's fall, Tim Harris, 'London Crowds and the Revolution of 1688' in Eveline Cruikshanks (ed.), *By Force or Default? The Revolution of 1688–1689* (Edinburgh, 1989).

Fonthill Abbey

The most recent book on Fonthill is the excellent Robert J. Gemmett, *Beckford's Fonthill: The Rise of a Romantic Icon* (Norwich, 2003); it has an exhaustive bibliography at the back. The catalogue of the 2001 Beckford Exhibition is excellent too and covers the breadth of his interests: Philip Hewat-Jaboor and Bet McLeod, *William Beckford, 1760–1844: An Eye for the Magnificent* (Yale, 2001). The most recent biography, not always reliable, but a brilliant read, is by Tim Mowl, *William Beckford: Composing for Mozart* (London, 1998); older but far from out of date and recently reprinted is James Lees Milne's essay, *William Beckford* (London, 1990). There is no really good biography of James Wyatt but the out-of-print book by John Martin Robinson, *The Wyatts: An architectural dynasty* (Oxford, 1979) has a section on him. Currently the best source is the third edition of Howard Colvin's *A Biographical Dictionary of British Architects* (Yale, 1995). A really good introduction to the Gothic revival is Megan Aldrich, *Gothic Revival* (London, 1999), and her bibliography provides pointers for those who want to dig deeper.

Theatre Royal, Drury Lane

There are two books on the Theatre Royal, Drury Lane, both out of print. The more modern is Brian Dobbs, *Drury Lane: Three Centuries of Theatre 1663–1971* (London, 1972) and the other is W. J. Macqueen Pope, *The Theatre Royal, Drury Lane* (London, 1945). Architecturally the *Survey of London* volume, *Theatre Royal, Drury Lane and the Royal Opera House, Covent Garden* (London, 1970) is the most useful publication to date, although Richard Leacroft, *The Development of the English Playhouse* (London, 1973) sets it in a wider context. None of the many books on Wren discuss the Drury Lane design in any depth, and the best architectural description of his work is still Kerry Downes, *The Architecture of Wren* (London, 1988). On Adam see Eileen Harris, *The Genius of Robert Adam: His Interiors* (Yale, 2001). There is an enormous literature of the seventeenth-

and eighteenth-century stage, and particularly on Garrick. Amongst the books I have found most useful are J. L. Styan, *Restoration Comedy in Performance* (Cambridge, 1986), Jean Benedetti, *David Garrick and the Birth of Modern Theatre* (London, 2001), Allardyce Nicholl, *The Garrick Stage: Theatre and Audience in the Eighteenth Century* (Manchester, 1980), Christopher Baugh, *Garrick and Loutherbourg* (Cambridge, 1990), Cecil Price, *Theatre in the Age of Garrick* (Oxford, 1973) and David Thomas (ed.), *Theatre in Europe: A Documentary History, Restoration and Georgian England 1660–1788* (Cambridge, 1989).

Nottingham Castle

The best (and only) book on Nottingham Castle is Christopher Drage, *Nottingham Castle: A Place Full Royal* (Nottingham, 1989). The Nottingham sections in H. M. Colvin (ed.), *The History of the King's Works*, 6 vols. (London, 1961–82) are equally valuable and cover the documentary evidence thoroughly. For a wider perspective of Nottingham, John Beckett, *A Centenary History of Nottingham* (Manchester, 1997) is very good. More generally Eric Ferney, *The Architecture of Norman England* (Oxford, 2002) is good on Norman castles, and his bibliography will point the curious further. On the political dimensions there is the out-of-print (but comprehensive) John Appleby, *England Without Richard 1189–1199* (London, 1965). Still in print is the gripping John Gillingham, *Richard I* (Yale, 2002). For more detail on Nottingham in the Richard–John struggle see the excellent article by Trevor Foulds, 'The Siege of Nottingham Castle in 1194', *Transactions of the Thoroton Society* XCV (1991). For the Parliamentary period a primary source that cannot be bettered is N. H. Keeble (ed.), *The memoirs of the Life of Colonel Hutchinson by his wife Lucy Hutchinson* (London, 1908). Finally, for Robin Hood see the recent S. Knight, *Robin Hood a Mythic Biography* (Ithaca, N. Y., 2003).

Millbank Penitentiary

The best modern books on prison architecture are Gillian Haggart (ed.), *Behind Closed Bars*: *The Hidden Architecture of England's Prisons* (London, 1999), Allan Brodie, Jane Croom and James O. Davies, *English Prisons*: *An Architectural History* (London, 2002) and Robin Evans, *The Fabrication of Virtue*: *English Prison Architecture 1750–1840* (Cambridge, 1982). However the best way to get to grips with Millbank is to attempt to track down some of the primary sources, all out of print, but all available with effort: Arthur Griffiths, *Memorials of Millbank & Chapters in Prison History* (London, 1875), George Peter Holford, *An Account of the General Penitentiary at Millbank* (London, 1828) and best of all, Chapter 5 of Mayhew & Binney, *Criminal Prisons of London* (London, 1862). More generally on crime and punishment see Sean McConville, *A History of English Prison Administration*, vol. I (London, 1981), M. Ignatieff, *A Just Measure of Pain*: *The Penitentiary in the Industrial Revolution, 1750–1850* (London, 1978) and Christopher Hibbert, *The Roots of Evil*: *A Social History of Crime and Punishment* (Harmondsworth, 1963).

Glastonbury Abbey

The best and only book on Glastonbury Abbey still in print is James P. Carley, *Glastonbury Abbey*: *The Holy House at the Head of the Moors Adventurous* (Woodbridge, 1996). Another good modern survey that takes in the wider context, but is out of print, is Philip Rahtz, *English Heritage Book of Glastonbury* (London, 1993). Peter Clery, *The Wealth and Estates of Glastonbury Abbey at the Dissolution in 1539* (Sutton Bridge, 2003) is an excellent snapshot of the abbey at its fall. This book should be read with Mick Aston's brilliant book, *Monasteries in the Landscape* (Stroud, 2002). Another book that throws specific light on Glastonbury is Robert Dunning, *Somerset Monasteries* (Stroud, 2001). Some general books on monasteries that are helpful are (in order of usefulness): Glyn Coppack, *English Heritage Book of Abbeys and Priories* (London, 1990); Colin Platt, *The Abbeys and Priories of Medieval England* (London, 1995);

Michael Thompson, *Cloister, Abbot and Precinct* (Stroud, 2001). On specific aspects of monastic life, see C. H. Lawrence, *Medieval Monasticism* (Harlow, 2001); R. C. Finucane, *Miracles and Pilgrims: Popular Beliefs in Medieval England* (London, 1977). On building the abbey, see Eric Fernie, *The Architecture of Norman England* (Oxford, 2000).

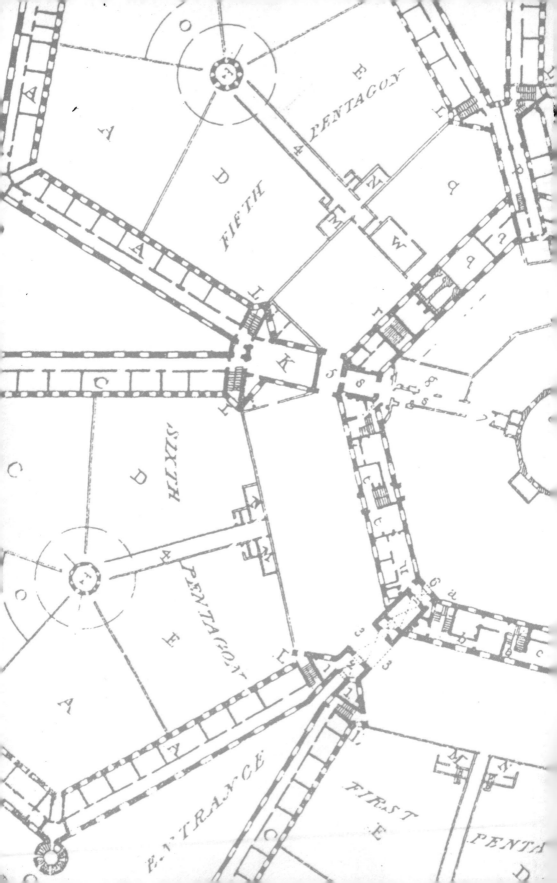